CAMP COCKTAILS

CAMP COCKTAILS

EASY, FUN & DELICIOUS DRINKS FOR THE GREAT OUTDOORS

EMILY VIKRE

HARVARD
COMMON
PRESS

First Published in 2020 by The Harvard Common Press, an imprint of The Quarto Group,
100 Cummings Center, Suite 265-D, Beverly, MA 01915, USA.
T (978) 282-9590 F (978) 283-2742 QuartoKnows.com

The Harvard Common Press titles are also available at discount for retail, wholesale, promotional, and bulk purchase. For details, contact the Special Sales Manager by email at specialsales@quarto.com or by mail at The Quarto Group, Attn: Special Sales Manager, 100 Cummings Center, Suite 265-D, Beverly, MA 01915, USA.

24 23 22 21 20   4 5

ISBN: 978-0-7603-6253-2

Digital edition published in 2020
eISBN: 978-0-7603-6254-9

Design: Amy Sly
Front Cover and Back Cover Images: Hanna Voxland and Emily Vikre
Page Layout: Amy Sly
Photography: Hanna Voxland and Emily Vikre

Library of Congress Cataloging-in-Publication Data

Names: Vikre, Emily, author.

Title: Camp cocktails: easy, fun, and delicious drinks for the great outdoors / Emily Vikre.

Description: Beverly: Harvard Common Press, 2020. | Includes index. | Summary: "Learn how to plan, pack, and whip up great drinks in the great outdoors. Cabin trips, hikes, patio parties, camping adventures-however you enjoy the great outdoors-it should be fun and easy. And so should the drinks! Simplicity, though, doesn't mean you're limited to a bottle and a mixer. With Camp Cocktails, you'll have a variety of options for simple and tasty drinks that are ready to go wherever you go. Cool off after a hot day spent hiking through the woods with a flask boulevardier or a Naglgene negroni. Break in the campsite with a grilled orange cobbler, blueberry-maple sparkler, or the ultimate beer-based cocktail. Bundling up around the fire? Warm up with the spiked Nutella hot chocolate, the penecillin toddy, or a boozy hot apple cider. Every recipe comes with easy-to-follow instructions, and many feature expert bartender tips and hacks. A variety of occasions are all here, from stargazing to boating. And to round it all out, there's a whole chapter dedicated to foraging/found ingredients, and integrating nature into your favorite cocktails"— Provided by publisher.

Identifiers: LCCN 2019024821 | ISBN 9780760362532 (hardcover)

Subjects: LCSH: Cocktails. | LCGFT: Cookbooks.

Classification: LCC TX951 .V513 2020 | DDC 641.87/4—dc23

LC record available at https://lccn.loc.gov/2019024821

Printed in China

The information in this book is for educational purposes only. It is not intended to replace the advice of a physician or medical practitioner. Please see your health-care provider before beginning any new health program.

FOR CHELSY AND SCUZZI,
MY FIRST — AND STILL
MY FAVORITE — COCKTAILING
COMPANIONS.

CONTENTS

INTRODUCTION

"This had better not turn into a goddamn expedition . . ."

Our family lore is filled with stories of, shall we say, character-building camping trips. Three-day trips in the pelting rain with nothing but roasted soy nuts to eat; weekends of climbing, sleeping on the wall, and eating only carrots and saltines; March ski camping trips that we thought would be warmer than they were (and so whole nights were spent sleepless, doing jumping jacks to get the circulation going again). The most memorable was a middle school trip, canoeing in the Boundary Waters with my parents and my two younger brothers. I say "canoeing," but as I recall, much of the trip was long portages or dragging the canoe through swamps too shallow to paddle through but too boggy to walk through easily. We crossed the top of a beaver dam, using it as a bridge, and my brothers' and my scrawny, gangly legs kept being swallowed by gaps in the beavers' handiwork and gashed by sharp stick ends. The kicker wasn't even the questionable route we were taking, though—it was that my parents had recently started us all on a macrobiotic diet and, as such, we didn't have real chocolate with us. We were forced to eat carob. Our neighbor, Sherry, when she first heard this story, laughed and said, "Oh yeah! We have a term for that in our family. We call them 'goddamn expeditions.'"

Now, it's not that my parents were bad at camping. It's that my dad believes in the sanctity of suffering. He probably wouldn't describe it as such, but it's obvious from watching him over the years that he takes a certain amount of pride in physical and mental strain, a sense that it purifies you and makes you a better person. It may be a Nordic thing. I know some of it has rubbed off on me because I catch myself in arguments with my husband, Joel, firmly telling him

that some unnecessarily uncomfortable thing is "good for us." His retort: "Well, this had better not turn into a goddamn expedition."

As I grew older, particularly after I moved to the East Coast, I learned that you could have a different approach to camping. I made friends who did things such as bring ingredients for Suzanne Goin's chorizo-pork burgers and a bottle of Bordeaux on a sea kayaking adventure; another who packed an eight-person tent and a queen-size blow-up mattress in her trunk just for herself when she went car camping; and others who rented tiny log huts in New Hampshire so we could stash an abundance of food and drink there, allowing us to climb up and ski down mountains by day, then feast at night. Escaping to the wilderness can be about pushing your physical and mental boundaries, but it can also be a celebration of the wild abundance of being alive on this gorgeous Earth, about the luxury of a slower pace and being fully present to yourself, your campmates, and your surroundings. And to me, there are few things quite as celebratory and convivial as a good cocktail.

Soon after I got into cocktails, my husband and I decided to leave our jobs in public health on the East Coast, move back to the northern shores of Lake Superior, and start a distillery, where we would make craft spirits that were a celebration of terroir, of the woods and water and culture of the area. Fun idea, right? It truly has been, although I'll also admit that entrepreneurship is its own kind of expedition. Two years in, a change in the laws allowed us to open a cocktail room at our distillery—that is to say, a bar where we could serve the spirits that we make. We went for it, and I began a deep dive into craft cocktails, history, cocktail technique,

and ingredients, including making some of my own new syrups and liqueurs with locally foraged plants (you'll find recipes for some of these in chapter 5!).

Somewhere along the way, I became the go-to person for planning and providing drinks for gatherings of all sorts, at our home, at weddings, at birthday parties, and even in the woods. And let me tell you, once you discover how amazing a craft cocktail tastes in the backwoods—or just outside on a back porch if you can't make it to the woods—you'll never want to go back to a plain old can of beer or flask of straight whiskey. That, in a nutshell, is the premise for this book. There is something about the balance and harmony of a good cocktail that mirrors the balance and harmony of nature. And the combination of the two, when the sun is at that golden angle, or the stars are a thick cascade across the sky, or you're by a crackling fire after a chilly day of hiking, can be transcendent.

HOW TO USE THIS BOOK

I've divided this book into chapters based on general styles of camping because how you're getting around and how much you can carry is going to have a massive influence on the types of cocktails you can make. I start with camping out of a backpack (or what I can't help but refer to as "real camping"). After this come recipes that you can add to your repertoire for car camping—that is, recipes that include citrus, soda, or things that you would bring in a cooler. Next come recipes for the cabin, or for "glamping," recipes that are less about roughing it and more about enjoying the spirit of relaxation and freedom that comes from the great outdoors. Finally, there is a chapter for bringing the outdoors inside by making things such as syrups, liqueurs, and bitters with foraged ingredients.

Because each chapter assumes you can have a slightly more complex setup than the last, you can certainly make

> "There is something about the balance and harmony of a good cocktail that mirrors the balance and harmony of nature."

any of the backpack camping recipes while car camping, or the car camping recipes at the cabin, and so on. Unless otherwise noted, the recipes make a single serving, but they are easy to scale up with a little math. Also, few of the recipes call for simple syrup because when you're camping it is easier to use a spoonful of sugar than to make a syrup. But, when you do see simple syrup called for (as in the cabin chapter), it is indeed incredibly simple to make. Just combine equal parts sugar and water (for example, ½ cup [100 g] sugar and ½ cup [120 ml] water), and stir until the sugar dissolves. You can do this over heat to make it go more quickly, but you don't have to.

I've included a wide range of recipes. Some are boozy, some light, some fruity, some bitter, some citrusy, and some herbal. Some are classic, and some are new inventions of mine. I've included drinks using aged spirits, clear spirits, and more. The unifying factor is that they are designed to be paired with wilderness, whether that's somewhere along the Appalachian Trail, near a lake deep in the Boundary Waters, in a cottage along the coast of Maine, or just the wildness of your own heart. And while they may be simplified for technique, they are all delicious enough that I am just as happy to make and drink them at home as I am in camp. No compromises.

And now it's time to raise a glass to getting outside!

Chapter One

BEFORE YOU LEAVE
(CAMP COCKTAIL BASICS)

HAVING A DRAM OF STRAIGHT WHISKEY BY THE CAMP-fire is a widely accepted part of camping. But enjoying a craft cocktail while on the trail? Maybe not. The idea of craft cocktails conjures up images of tattooed, mustachioed bartenders, delicate barware, and absinthe in atomizers. We go to the woods to escape, to find a simpler way of being . . . Aren't craft cocktails antithetical to that experience?

In my opinion, no. We get out of doors and away from our regular lives to simplify and clarify our minds, but not to simplify our sensory experience. If anything, we seek to deepen our sensory experience. To breathe in the smell of morning mist, pine trees, and campfire smoke. To soak in the color of wild-flowers and sunsets. To actually hear birdsong and the gossiping chatter of red squirrels. If we are delighting all of our other senses by being outside, why would we compromise that by eating or drinking something sort of terrible?!

In the world of cooking, we have moved away from surviving off of frankfurters and dehydrated cheesy rice at the campsite, and made gourmet camp food a thing. It's time for our drinking to catch up.

Maybe you already bring beer with you, or a box of wine. But there is something special about enjoying a nice cocktail when you're in camp. No matter what is going on, a good cocktail turns the moment into a celebration, which is exactly the right mood to create after a long day of paddling or when you've finally gotten away from the city to enjoy a weekend with old friends, or new friends, your kids, your siblings . . .

There may be several reasons why cocktails are so celebratory, but one I think about a lot is simply the fact that it takes a little extra effort to serve a cocktail. With good wine or beer, the effort is backloaded. The winemaker or brewer put a lot of work into their craft and produced something delicious that you can open and enjoy. With a cocktail, the effort is backloaded *and* frontloaded! Not only has a lot of work gone into producing the fine ingredients in the cocktail, but the person making the cocktail is also adding an extra layer of care, and consequently specialness, by combining the ingredients just so to make a drink that elevates the ordinary to something extraordinary.

So, yes, there's a little extra effort involved if you want to enjoy a cocktail. But, it doesn't have to be an intimidating amount of effort. Many of the greatest cocktails require just

two or three ingredients. Many use ingredients you already have anyway. Many can be prepared at home and brought with you, ready to enjoy at a moment's notice. This book will give you the tools for all of these options and then some.

First, let's start with some basics you'll need to know.

TRANSPORTING SPIRITS

You can't make a cocktail in the wilderness if you don't bring cocktail ingredients, and you'll want to be sure you're transporting your spirits safely. The best way to do this, however, depends on how you're getting around. When fitting everything into a backpack, you'll want to transfer your spirits into lightweight, leakproof, nonbreakable containers, and you'll

want to focus on choosing just one, maybe two things to bring (which is not to say I haven't lugged a carefully packed bottle of Champagne in a pack through the Presidential Mountains, because I sure have, but that was a very special occasion).

I'm a big fan of the tried-and-true water bottle for a long or group trip. The bottle is 1 liter, so it's big enough to hold

more than a whole 750 ml bottle of spirits, or about eight full-size servings of a cocktail. You can also transfer spirits or premixed cocktails into flasks, collapsible bladders that are made for holding liquid, or other water bottles that seal well. If you're choosing a flask for camping, you can find lightweight ones made of plastic-like material, or you can choose good old-fashioned stainless steel. Both work great. Just make sure you clean your flask out well as soon as you get home. I like to fill mine with boiling water, drain it, and dry it. To get it extra clean you can use a 1:1 mixture of water and white vinegar for soaking it. Then give it an extra rinse of boiling hot water to get rid of any vinegar residue.

If you're car camping or headed to the cabin, you can use any of these methods, or you could transport whole bottles. Put glass bottles in a sturdy box or crate to keep them from rattling around. Wedge your dishtowel(s) between any bottles for extra security. And make sure that when you're driving, any alcohol is in your trunk, so that you don't accidentally violate open container laws. And always, always remember that anything you bring into a park or campsite with you should leave the park or campsite with you. Pack it in, pack it out.

COCKTAIL TECHNIQUE

They say a novelist needs a foundation of proper grammar and knowledge of the three-point essay so they can then break the rules with finesse. Likewise, you need to know proper cocktail-making tools and technique so that you can draw on that knowledge to MacGyver a good cocktail in the woods without the luxury of a perfect bar setup. This is not a cocktail basics book, however, so I'll keep it quick and simple. (If you want to get a more intense primer on cocktail technique, my two favorite books are *The Bar Book* by Jeffrey Morgenthaler and the first several chapters of *Death & Co* by David Kaplan, Nick Fauchald, and Alex Day.)

MEASURING

Measure each ingredient for your cocktail precisely. "Do I really need to measure?" you may ask. Yes! You do. Okay, so you don't necessarily need to measure if you're making the kind of cocktail I call a "blank and blank" (such as vodka and soda, gin and tonic, rum and cola), where you are adding a shot or so of spirit to an already made mixer. But for all other cocktails, do yourself a favor and measure. Cocktails are more like baking than cooking. They require precision for the flavors to really click into place. Why? Cocktail ingredients have their own set of nuanced and complex flavors, so to combine complex flavor profiles in a way that's greater than the sum of their parts, you have to get the balance right.

I usually work in ounces for measuring liquids when making cocktails, mainly because that's what I'm used to and is the type of jigger we use in our bar. If you prefer to use kitchen measurements, here are a couple of handy conversions to know: there are 2 tablespoons in 1 ounce (30 ml), and there are 4 tablespoons in a ¼ cup (60 ml), meaning ¼ cup is 2 ounces (60 ml). If you use metric, the conversion to keep in mind is that 1 ounce equals 30 ml. In this book, I use mainly ounces for fluid measurements, and for dry ingredients I use tablespoons and cups.

STIRRING

When you stir a cocktail, the goal is to combine the ingredients and allow the ice to properly dilute and chill the cocktail without incorporating any extra air into the drink. The perfect texture for a stirred cocktail is like icy cold silk. To stir a cocktail, first measure your ingredients into a stirring vessel. Carefully add ice, trying not to splash it in (remember, we're avoiding adding air!), then stir by moving your stirring utensil

pulling the shaker toward you with a quick, almost jerking, motion. Quickly push the shaker away from you, parallel to the floor, in a shallow arc, then pull it back, and so forth. You are trying to move the ice all the way from one end of the shaker to the other in an elliptical motion inside the shaker. An elliptical motion is better than straight back and forth because it means the ice is less likely to totally shatter.

The particulars of someone's perfect shaking motion tend to be peculiar just to them (in some cases very peculiar!). You'll see top bartenders with different shaking techniques, but the fundamentals of what is happening inside the shaker are the same. You can experiment to develop your own stylish yet comfortable shaking technique—over your shoulder? Right in front of you? In an ellipse or with a V shape going back and forth?—as long as you are shaking with vigor. You want to shake until the cocktail is well chilled and properly diluted. How long this takes will depend on a number of factors,

smoothly around the inside wall of your stirring vessel. If you stir smoothly you can create a sort of liquid vortex, so it moves around without sloshing. After stirring for about 15 to 20 seconds, pause and take a small taste of the cocktail to see whether it is diluted to your liking. If it is, stop and strain the cocktail into your drinking glass. If it still tastes too hot, meaning the alcohol burn is stronger than you like, keep stirring for 5 to 10 seconds longer, then strain.

SHAKING

When you shake a cocktail, the goal is to combine the ingredients while also aerating them, giving the cocktail a lightness, even fluffiness, as well as to chill and dilute the cocktail. To shake a cocktail, measure your ingredients into a shaker, add ice, and close the shaker (I'll talk a little more about different shakers in the barware section). Pick up the shaker. Grab it with one hand around the middle, and use the other hand to support the side that is away from you. Start shaking by either a Hawthorne strainer or a more specialized strainer called a julep strainer that looks like a metal bowl with little holes in it and a handle. Fit a julep strainer snugly at an angle into your stirring vessel and strain through it. A julep strainer is nice for stirred drinks because it keeps them extra silky, but it isn't necessary.

Double straining is often called for when you're making a cocktail that contains muddled ingredients, tiny pieces of which might slip through the coils of the Hawthorne strainer. When you double strain, you pour through your cocktail strainer and through a fine-mesh strainer held above your cocktail glass. You can buy really nice conical fine-mesh strainers specifically for cocktails, or you can just use a small mesh kitchen strainer or even a tea strainer.

and it takes practice to start to be able to sense when the cocktail is ready. You'll be able to feel it getting cold, and hear that the ice pieces have started to sound smaller than they were before. It usually takes about 12 to 15 seconds. Open the shaker and strain the cocktail into your cocktail glass.

STRAINING

You strain a cocktail so your final drink will have a uniform texture, without ice chunks or bits of ingredients that were muddled into the cocktail. At a bar, you strain a cocktail even if it is going to be served over ice. When I'm camping, I often skip the straining step because having ice at all is already a luxury.

But when you have a full bar setup, use a Hawthorne strainer for shaken drinks. This is the style of strainer that is a flat metal disk with a handle attached to one side and a coiled spring around the underside of the metal disk. The coiled spring fits snugly against your shaker and strains out any bits of ice or fruit or herbs. For a stirred drink you can use

CAMP-FRIENDLY BARWARE

Now that we have a sense of the basic techniques for making cocktails, we can see what equipment we really need, like *need* need, for making them. At a minimum, you need something to measure with, something to shake and/or stir in, something to stir with, something to strain with (maybe), and something to drink out of. You'll also need a small sharp knife for things such as cutting small bits of citrus peel, but this is something you should have with you when you are camping anyway, or you're really going to have trouble sharpening sticks for roasting marshmallows. Here's what you'll want on hand.

SOMETHING TO MEASURE WITH

The standard for measuring ingredients for cocktails is a jigger. These are the little things that look like two metal cones attached at their tips in an hourglass shape. Jiggers are small and sturdy, so if you've decided you're going to make cocktails in camp, there's not much reason not to pack one in your kitchen kit. If you get a jigger, the most useful kinds are the ones that have little etched measuring lines inside. A stainless steel "Japanese-style 1-ounce/2-ounces" jigger that has ½-, ¾-, and 1½-ounce measurement markings, in addition to 1 and 2 ounces, is awesome. One of my favorite tools for measuring cocktail ingredients is actually a ¼-cup measuring cup (I have two of them because one is always dirty, I use them that often). It has all the measurement markings, is lightweight, and has a little pouring spout, a boon for someone like me who is prone to spilling. And, as I mentioned before, you can use a tablespoon for measuring, if you remember that 1 tablespoon is ½ ounce (15 ml).

SOMETHING TO STIR OR SHAKE WITH

Stirring is easy. Yes, you can stir in a beautiful etched glass Japanese stirring vessel, which is specially designed to facilitate smooth stirring and cold retention. Or you can just stir in anything that holds liquid. You can stir right in your camp cup because you are camping, and you want a cocktail now. You can also use any variety of utensils for stirring. A long, twisted-handle barspoon is lovely and beautifully weighted for a perfectly smooth stirring motion. But you know what else works great for smooth stirring? A spoon handle, a knife, a chopstick, your finger . . .

Shaking is only a little trickier. For shaking, you need a vessel that will close tightly so that no liquid spills out while you shake. My go-to at the bar is a tin-on-tin Boston shaker. This

is the type of shaker that comes as two pint glass–shaped tins, one a little smaller than the other. To use one, build your cocktail in the smaller of the two tins, add ice, and then cover with the larger of the two tins. Fit the larger tin over at an angle so that along one side of the shaker you have a straight line up and down, then bop the top with the palm of your hand to seal. Pick up the shaker, bringing the smaller tin toward you, and start shaking. To break the seal between the two tins, find the side of the shaker that is 90 degrees from the side where the two tins form a straight line, then whack it with the heel of your palm and the seal should release. This type of Boston shaker is cheap, lightweight, and durable, plus one tin slips right inside the other, and your jigger slips right inside of that, so you could bring it with you if you're car camping, heading to the cabin, or even canoeing if you have gourmet plans for your weekend. Don't forget your strainer.

The cobbler shaker is the kind of metal shaker that is tapered at the top, has a built-in strainer, and has a little met-

al cap that goes over that. The built-in strainer is convenient for traveling, but, personally, I loathe this kind of shaker. In the vast majority of them, the metal gets cold and contracts as you shake, and I can never—never!—get the darn little cap to come off without a lot of banging and cursing. You can find insulated cobbler shakers specifically designed to avert this problem. However, the thermos manufacturer Stanley makes a camping bar kit that has an insulated shaker that basically follows the design of a cobbler shaker, but the cap *screws* on and off, and doubles as a measuring jigger. Clever.

You can also totally make use of nonspecialized containers for shaking, as long as they seal. Shake your cocktail in a thermos—the kind where you then press a little button at the top to allow you to pour out of it basically has its own built-in strainer as well! Or shake in a water bottle or a jar with a tight-sealing lid. To be honest, when I'm at home or camping out of a car, I rarely bother with a cocktail shaker. Instead, I use a mason jar because I always have them around.

SOMETHING TO STRAIN WITH

You can strain with anything that will act as a barrier to hold back ice and little bits of ingredients while still letting you pour liquid. If you don't want to pack a cocktail strainer or a shaker with a built-in strainer, you can strain through your thermos or water bottle opening. You can hold a jar lid, another small lid, or a plate against your shaking or stirring vessel and slide it to the side to open just a crack. You can also use a small kitchen strainer if you brought one of those.

SOMETHING TO MUDDLE WITH

If a recipe calls for muddling, you don't need a specialized muddler either. You can use the handle of a wooden spoon, the bowl of a regular spoon or spork, or any other slightly heavy, fairly smooth object.

SOMETHING TO DRINK OUT OF

The world is full of gorgeous, drink-specific glasses with shapes and weights to enhance the flavors of your drink. Don't worry about these. Just pour your cocktail into whatever cup you have with you. It will taste perfect. Or drink it straight from the flask or water bottle. That is absolutely part of the fun. If you want to be a cool cat, Stanley makes lightweight metal cocktail tumblers for camping, or you can get a set of lightweight metal shot glasses that come in their own carrying case. I have a set because they were too cute to resist. You can also find clear plastic stemless wineglasses that are durable, light, and quite classy looking.

LET'S TALK ABOUT ICE

Ice is a critical cocktail ingredient, and one you may or may not have access to when you're camping (at the cabin and at home I do assume you have ice readily available). Ice serves several purposes in a cocktail: First, it dilutes the cocktail. When you have a well-made cocktail, 20 to 25 percent of its volume is actually water that was added by shaking or stirring it with ice. Next, ice chills the cocktail, and a chilled cocktail tastes smoother and more drinkable. Finally, ice emulsifies the ingredients together in a shaken cocktail. If you have good ice, great! Use it to shake and stir as you normally would. "Good ice" is ice that is very cold, very hard, and free

of any off smells. More likely is that you'll either have cooler ice or no ice at all.

If you can avoid it, don't use the same cooler ice for chilling your food and for making cocktails. It will likely have bad flavors and odors. I recommend freezing a bunch of large ice cubes—for example 2-inch (5 cm) cubes—or even freezing a baking pan filled with water (dip the outside briefly in very hot water to loosen the edges so that you can take the big ice chunk out), or freezing whole zip-top bags filled with water, to make large ice cubes. Seal your large ice cubes in a double layer of zip-top bags and stash them along the side of your cooler. If you are able to, you can even bring a second cooler that is just for cocktail ice and drink ingredients. This way, you don't have your drinks by the chicken kabobs that you're planning to grill, and you're not opening the cocktail cooler as often because you're not rummaging in it for breakfast and lunch. When you use the ice you've packed for cocktails, scoop it out and do your best to shake or drain off the water accumulating around it. The smaller the pieces of ice are, the harder but faster you want to stir or shake your cocktail.

If you have no ice at all, make sure you dilute your cocktail with some water, to approximate the dilution effect you would get from shaking or stirring. Do a little math to calculate 20 to 25 percent of the cocktail volume and add that on top of your cocktail. Then, you can put it in a water bottle or flask and, if it's possible, go stick that container into cold water, such as a stream or lake, to chill it. If you're winter camping, chilling is easy, but you may prefer to warm up with a hot cocktail anyway. And speaking of hot cocktails, they are one of the simplest work-arounds for not having ice. Who is going to miss a chilled martini when they're sipping on a steaming, boozy hot toddy anyway?

Chapter Two

BACKPACKING

MY HUSBAND, JOEL, AND I HAD BEEN TRUDGING uphill through increasingly loose packed snow for two hours before we finally admitted that we had taken a wrong turn. We scrutinized our topo map and, after some head scratching and swearing, figured out where we had gone wrong. The good news was there was a way to connect back with the main trail. The bad news was that it involved a climb over a small snowy mountain. But it was still shorter than heading back the way we came, so we set off again. What was intended to be an easy afternoon loop from our camp turned into a seven-hour slog. The last rays of the sun disappeared as we stumbled back out onto the well-packed main trail. We fished our headlamps out of our breast pockets and, as tired as we were, jubilantly jogged the last half hour of gently sloping downhill back to the trailhead. Back in camp, we changed into dry long underwear and started on dinner. Macaroni and cheese with a side of whiskey-spiked hot chocolate has never tasted better.

Whether you're backpacking, backcountry skiing, canoeing, kayaking, or climbing, you are probably trying to streamline your packing list and reduce weight. But streamlined does not need to be synonymous with Spartan. A nip of a well-crafted cocktail while you're boiling water for dinner or meditating by the campfire tastes luxurious. And after working hard all day, you've earned it. Plus, as my friend Jake, who owns an outdoor adventure guiding company, says, "When we pack for trips, we try to bring only things that have at least two uses. And alcohol is also a disinfectant! So have at it!"

FLASK COCKTAILS

The easiest way to have a balanced cocktail when you're camping? Balance it at home with all the luxury of multiple bottles and measuring utensils, then funnel it into a flask to carry with you. By "flask," I mean any container made to carry liquid and seal well. You could use an actual flask, but if you prefer you could also use a water bottle, or thermos, or a plastic reservoir used in hydration packs. Whatever you choose for transporting your cocktail of choice, here are a few flask-building principles to abide by.

1. **Use good-quality spirits.** Yes, you might be able to chill your flask cocktail in a cool lake or a snowbank depending on when and where you are camping, but you should be prepared to drink your cocktail at the ambient air temperature; at warmer temperatures any harshness or imbalance in the booze becomes more apparent.

2. **Opt for an aged spirit as your base spirit.** This is not a hard-and-fast rule. Some people may be totally happy to have a gin cocktail from a flask, but I find that aged spirits (aka brown spirits) are softer and rounder in flavor from the process of aging in oak, and this makes them more pleasant at room temperature.

3. **Choose a "stirred" cocktail recipe.** You want to choose a recipe with all booze-based ingredients. A syrup is okay, but I mainly opt for recipes that call for liqueurs instead of syrups. Avoid citrus, dairy, and egg. You want all of the ingredients in your cocktail to be super stable so that they don't degrade over the time spent together in the flask and at room temperature.

4. **Choose a recipe that is interesting but that you'll be happy sipping several nights in a row.** I say choose something interesting because you want your flask cocktails to be complex enough, even challenging enough, that they give you a full sensory experience with just a few sips. Why? Because you're out on the trail, working hard, making good decisions, and being safe, and this is not the time to go crazy, even once your tent is staked for the night. I always choose a cocktail that is on the bitter and moody side for that reason. That said, you don't want to fill a flask to last four nights only to find that after one night of enjoying your dram you're totally over it and wishing for something else.

5. **Do some math!** You can convert any recipe to fit any size carrying vessel with a little math. Get ready to become friends with ratios and percentages. The basic method is: add up all of the individual ingredient volumes to get the total volume of one serving. If you want to have your cocktail prediluted, which I recommend because it really helps with softening and opening up the flavors of the drink, calculate 20 to 25 percent of the cocktail volume. That's your water volume. Add this to the total volume. Then use this new total volume to figure out how many times you need to multiply your recipe to fit the size container you want to use.

Also, bitters don't always scale proportionally. The bigger the batch, the less predictable it is. When I multiply a recipe, I start by using only half the amount of bitters that I calculate and then add more to taste. Got that? Me either.

Let's practice some batching math. Start with a Manhattan. The recipe I like to use is 2½ ounces (75 ml) whiskey, 1 ounce (30 ml) sweet vermouth, and 2 dashes of bitters. Thus, 2½ + 1 = 3½ ounces (105 ml) total; the bitters don't count toward the volume because the amounts are too small. Next, 20 percent of 3½ ounces (105 ml) is 0.7 ounce (21 ml), which is an awkward amount, so we will up that slightly to 0.75 (or ¾) ounce (23 ml) of water. Add this in and your total volume of the finished cocktail is 4¼ ounces (128 ml). If you have an

8-ounce (240 ml) flask, you won't be able to quite fit two servings of cocktail. You can deal with this in two potential ways. The easiest thing to do is make a double batch (5 ounces [150 ml] whiskey, 2 ounces [60 ml] sweet vermouth, 4 dashes of bitters, and 1½ ounces [45 ml] water), funnel what fits into your flask, and then save or drink the small amount remaining. Or you could make a one and three-quarters batch, in which case you would multiply each of the ingredient amounts by 1.75 and deal with the awkward amounts. See, this is why I put that exclamation point after do some math! Phew. Don't worry. I'll also give you batch measurements in the recipes in this chapter.

FLASK MANHATTAN

I have a deep affection for Manhattans, even the bad ones. It is my lazy evening cocktail, the only cocktail I make without measuring because I like the combination of whiskey and vermouth (plus a dash of bitters) in any proportion. It is a winning combo. The Manhattan debuted on the cocktail scene in the 1870s and has reigned, unquestioned and timeless, ever since. While I am an equal opportunity Manhattan drinker, some renditions are discernably better than others, and because you're going to the trouble of preparing a flask ahead of time, why not have the best?

FOR 1 COCKTAIL

2½ ounces (75 ml) rye or bourbon whiskey

1 ounce (30 ml) sweet vermouth

2 dashes Angostura bitters

¾ ounce (23 ml) water

FOR AN 8-OUNCE (240 ML) FLASK

5 ounces (150 ml) whiskey

2 ounces (60 ml) vermouth

4 dashes Angostura bitters

1½ ounces (45 ml) water

FOR A 32-OUNCE (960 ML) WATER BOTTLE

18¾ ounces (563 ml) whiskey

7½ ounces (225 ml) vermouth

10 dashes Angostura bitters

5½ ounces (165 ml) water

Combine all the ingredients, stir gently to combine, and pour or funnel all, or all that fits, into your carrying vessel.

CHANGE IT UP! The Manhattan has some easy and equally wonderful variations that are, if anything, even better suited to camping. To make a Rob Roy, simply use blended Scotch as your whiskey and keep everything else the same as for a Manhattan. To make a Bobby Burns, use a Highland malt Scotch as your whiskey, and instead of 2 dashes of bitters, add a barspoon of Bénédictine for each serving.

FLASK BRANDY AND BÉNÉDICTINE

I don't know anyone for whom a B&B (short for brandy and Bénédictine) is a go-to cocktail. I suspect that for most, if the cocktail conjures up any mental association, it's an image of a tweedy grandfatherly type, who may be charming in his own way but whose tastes are pain-fully outmoded. This is a shame because the honeyed tones of brandy and Bénédictine are warm, herbal, and complex. It makes me think of a walk through autumn leaves on a crisp, sunny day. All that the B&B needs is a little proportion updating to make it perfect. Instead of the classic 1:1 ratio, I dial back the amount of Bénédictine. This dries up the cocktail, making it more drinkable, and tones down the herb flavors to keep them from reading as medicinal. Make sure you choose a nice brandy—I favor a VSOP cognac—because it is the linchpin of the cocktail.

FOR 1 COCKTAIL
2 ounces (60 ml) cognac

½ ounce (15 ml) Bénédictine

½ ounce (15 ml) water

FOR AN 8-OUNCE (240 ML) FLASK
5 ounces (150 ml) cognac

1¼ ounces (38 ml) Bénédictine

1¼ ounces (38 ml) water

FOR A 32-OUNCE (960 ML) WATER BOTTLE
20 ounces (600 ml) cognac

5 ounces (150 ml) Bénédictine

5 ounces (150 ml) water

Combine all the ingredients, stir gently to combine, and pour or funnel all, or all that fits, into your carrying vessel.

FLASK VIEUX CARRÉ

If you mash up a Manhattan (page 31) and a B&B (page 32), boom! You have a Vieux Carré. This is one of my husband's favorite cocktails, but he can never remember the name of it. Nevertheless, it's an amazing fireside drink. The silky texture and interesting but approachable flavor are the perfect complement to watching sparks crackle and float up toward a sky carpeted with stars.

FOR 1 COCKTAIL

¾ ounce (23 ml) rye whiskey

¾ ounce (23 ml) cognac

¾ ounce (23 ml) sweet vermouth

1 teaspoon (5 ml) Bénédictine

1 dash Peychaud's bitters

1 dash Angostura bitters

½ ounce (15 ml) water

FOR AN 8-OUNCE (240 ML) FLASK

2 ounces (60 ml) rye whiskey

2 ounces (60 ml) cognac

2 ounces (60 ml) sweet vermouth

2½ teaspoons (13 ml) Bénédictine

2 dashes Peychaud's bitters

2 dashes Angostura bitters

1½ ounces (45 ml) water

FOR A 32-OUNCE (960 ML) WATER BOTTLE

8 ounces (240 ml) rye whiskey

8 ounces (240 ml) cognac

8 ounces (240 ml) sweet vermouth

1¾ ounces (53 ml) Bénédictine

7 dashes Peychaud's bitters

7 dashes Angostura bitters

6 ounces (180 ml) water

Combine all the ingredients, stir gently to combine, and pour or funnel all, or all that fits, into your carrying vessel.

CHANGE IT UP! For your summer kayaking and canoe trips, try giving the Vieux Carré a tropical spin, like I've seen from the bar Drink in Boston, by using Plantation pineapple rum in place of the cognac.

"RUM AND COLA" OLD FASHIONED

In a case of extreme misnomers, neither is this an Old Fashioned nor does it contain any cola. But the first time I made it I mused to myself, "This tastes kind of like an Old Fashioned made with rum and cola," and the name stuck. If you know your cocktails and you look closely, the 1:1:1 ratio will actually give it away as a Negroni riff. And like a Negroni, it is brash and boldly flavored. Sometimes this is just what the doctor ordered. It will certainly fire your legs back up when they're fatigued from a day of touring. But if you find you prefer a more delicate cocktail balance, you can make it with 1½ parts rum and ¾ part each of sweet vermouth and Averna.

FOR 1 COCKTAIL

1 ounce (30 ml) aged Spanish-style rum

1 ounce (30 ml) sweet vermouth

1 ounce (30 ml) Averna amaro

1 dash Angostura bitters

¾ ounce (23 ml) water

FOR AN 8-OUNCE (240 ML) FLASK

2 ounces (60 ml) aged Spanish-style rum

2 ounces (60 ml) sweet vermouth

2 ounces (60 ml) Averna amaro

2 dashes Angostura bitters

1½ ounces (45 ml) water

FOR A 32-OUNCE (960 ML) WATER BOTTLE

8½ ounces (255 ml) aged Spanish-style rum

8½ ounces (255 ml) sweet vermouth

8½ ounces (255 ml) Averna amaro

6 dashes Angostura bitters

6¼ ounces (188 ml) water

Combine all the ingredients, stir gently to combine, and pour or funnel all, or all that fits, into your carrying vessel.

A Flask of Amaro

Because I firmly believe that flask cocktails should be a little moody and a little bitter-sweet, you'll see many of them include at least one type of amaro. Amari (plural of amaro) are bittersweet, herbal digestive liqueurs, usually from Italy. They can range from very bitter, such as Fernet and Cynar, to a much gentler bitterness, such as Averna and Nonino. I love them all and think they add an incomparable complexity to cocktails. But I think my very favorite is Nonino (full name: Amaro Nonino Quintessentia, which would also be the name of my cat if I had one). Nonino has incredibly easygoing notes of marmalade and saffron and is so well balanced that sipping it straight is basically like sipping a ready-made cocktail. So, sometimes I fill my flask with just that. Plus, it tastes great in hot cocoa.

FLASK BOULEVARDIER

The Negroni was the cocktail that first made me fall in love with craft cocktails. I've loved Campari since, well, since an earlier age than was appropriate for me to love Campari. And the combination of gin, Campari, and sweet vermouth is undeniably a classic. It's also undeniably not very good at room temperature. I keep trying flask Negronis, but they are always a disappointment. The interplay of gin and Campari is too harsh when it isn't perfectly chilled. So what's a Negroni-loving girl to do for her camping trips? The solution is simple: make one of the many Negroni variations that use an aged base spirit. The most well known is the Boulevardier, which marries the bittersweet Campari and vermouth with the lush oak of bourbon.

FOR 1 COCKTAIL

2 ounces (60 ml) bourbon

1 ounce (30 ml) Campari

1 ounce (30 ml) sweet vermouth

1 ounce (30 ml) water

FOR AN 8-OUNCE (240 ML) FLASK

3½ ounces (105 ml) bourbon

1¾ ounces (53 ml) Campari

1¾ ounces (53 ml) sweet vermouth

1¾ ounces (53 ml) water

FOR A 32-OUNCE (960 ML) WATER BOTTLE

12½ ounces (375 ml) bourbon

6¼ ounces (188 ml) Campari

6¼ ounces (188 ml) sweet vermouth

6¼ ounces (188 ml) water

Combine all the ingredients, stir gently to combine, and pour or funnel all, or all that fits, into your carrying vessel.

CHANGE IT UP! Try the cocktail with apple brandy instead of bourbon. It gives the drink a little extra softness without making it overtly fruity. Or, if you find wild raspberries while you are in the woods, crush some in a camp cup and pour some of your Boulevardier over them. Raspberries and Campari have an unlikely but beautiful flavor friendship.

SHETLAND SWEATER

Scotland is renowned for its whisky. It is also renowned for inclement weather. My friend Dave Pagel, who is also an outdoor writer, once told me a story of hiking in Scotland through pelting rain and biting wind. As he struggled up a steep cliff, soaked with sweat and the rain seeping through his cuffs and collar, he came upon a man strolling along buck naked, but for a woolen cap and a sturdy umbrella. As their paths crossed they had a brief, surprisingly cheerful inter-change. Dave couldn't help but remark on the man's extremely, one could say excessively, natural state of dress. The man replied in a sage brogue, "There's nae escapin' the rain. In weather such as this ye can be wet inside and oot . . . or just oot." And away he went. There is wisdom in his words, but still, let us hope that after he returned to shelter he warmed himself up with both a fuzzy sweater and a smooth, hearty cocktail like this one.

FOR 1 COCKTAIL
1 ounce (30 ml) blended Scotch

½ ounce (15 ml) Laird's bonded applejack

½ ounce (15 ml) Averna amaro

½ ounce (15 ml) Amaro Nonino

½ teaspoon maple syrup

1 dash orange bitters

a generous ½ ounce (15 ml) water

FOR AN 8-OUNCE (240 ML) FLASK
3 ounces (90 ml) blended Scotch

1½ ounces (45 ml) Laird's bonded applejack

1½ ounces (45 ml) Averna amaro

1½ ounces (45 ml) Amaro Nonino

1½ teaspoons (8 ml) maple syrup

2 dashes orange bitters

1½ ounces (45 ml) water

FOR A 32-OUNCE (960 ML) WATER BOTTLE
10½ ounces (315 ml) blended Scotch

5¼ ounces (158 ml) Laird's bonded applejack

5¼ ounces (158 ml) Averna amaro

5¼ ounces (158 ml) Amaro Nonino

¾ ounce (23 ml) maple syrup

6 dashes orange bitter

5¼ ounces (158 ml) water

Combine all ingredients, stir gently to combine, and pour or funnel all, or all that fits, into your carrying vessel.

SCAFFA

The scaffa is a category of spirituous mixed drink almost completely lost to history because as ice became more readily available, the chilled and diluted cocktail became the norm. But before the rise of affordable ice in the mid-nineteenth century, drinks were usually served at room tempera- ture or hot, and often without the softening addition of water (water was a key ingredient in defining what was called a "cocktail" in the 1800s).

So, a scaffa is a drink composed of mixed spirits and liqueurs, sometimes bitters, that is intended to be served unchilled and undiluted. Sounds like a perfect fit for a flask to me. The term scaffa may have come from the old English word for "cupboard" because these drinks could have been mixed from whatever was lying around in the cupboard. Even if that were the case, I'd suggest a much more careful approach. Because there is no chilling or diluting, the balance of flavors in a scaffa is a delicate science and many of the historic scaffa recipes I found and tested tasted awful. So, I took matters into my own hands and invented this cocktail, focusing on the flavor interplay of spicy rye and the menthol and chocolate of Amaro Nardini, which is a combination I love.

FOR DRINK

1½ ounces (45 ml) sweet vermouth

¾ ounce (23 ml) rye whiskey

¼ ounce (8 ml) dry curaçao (I like Pierre Ferrand Dry Curaçao but you could also use another good orange liqueur such as Cointreau)

¼ ounce (8 ml) Amaro Nardini

FOR AN 8-OUNCE (240 ML) FLASK

4½ ounces (135 ml) sweet vermouth

2¼ ounces (68 ml) rye whiskey

¾ ounce (23 ml) dry curaçao

¾ ounce (23 ml) Amaro Nardini

FOR A 32-OUNCE (960 ML) WATER BOTTLE

18 ounces (540 ml) sweet vermouth

9 ounces (270 ml) rye whiskey

3 ounces (90 ml) dry curaçao

3 ounces (90 ml) Amaro Nardini

Combine all the ingredients, stir gently to combine, and pour or funnel all, or all that fits, into your carrying vessel.

MAGIA OSCURA

Of all the many cocktails in this book, this may be my very favorite for capping off a day on the trail. To me, it is the epitome of an outdoor nightcap. It's inspired by the Hanky Panky, a Prohibition-era gin cocktail (in the 1920s, hanky-panky referred to dark magic not to, ahem, what we now think of as hanky-panky). Mezcal and Fernet Branca are both challenging ingredients, the one aggressively smoky, the other aggressively bitter. But when you bring them together with a bridge of sweet vermouth, they become surprisingly smooth, even at room temperature. The mezcal wafts notes of campfire smoke, and the Fernet tastes distinctly earthy, like a mouthful of forest floor . . . a pleasant mouthful, though. It tastes just like an evening in camp, and I like that about it.

FOR 1 COCKTAIL

1½ ounces (45 ml) mezcal

1½ ounces (45 ml) sweet vermouth

¼ ounce (8 ml) Fernet Branca

¾ ounce (23 ml) water

FOR AN 8-OUNCE (240 ML) FLASK

3 ounces (90 ml) mezcal

3 ounces (90 ml) sweet vermouth

½ ounce (15 ml) Fernet Branca

1½ ounces (45 ml) water

FOR A 32-OUNCE (960 ML) WATER BOTTLE

12 ounces (360 ml) mezcal

12 ounces (360 ml) sweet vermouth

2 ounces (60 ml) Fernet Branca

6 ounces (180 ml) water

Combine all ingredients, stir gently to combine, and pour or funnel all, or all that fits, into your carrying vessel.

Easy "Spikeables"

NO MATTER HOW LIGHT YOU'RE TRAVELING,
as long as you have a nip of booze in a flask, you're bound
to have some ingredients with you that you can transform
into a cocktail. (When you have a hammer, everything looks
like a nail. When you have bourbon, everything looks like a
cocktail. As they say.) Although anything tastes good after a
long day on the trail, these cocktails taste especially good.

CAMPSITE "IRISH COFFEE"

5 ounces (150 ml) strong hot coffee or 1 packet of instant coffee mixed with 5 ounces (150 ml) hot water

1 tablespoon (15 g) brown sugar

1 ounce (30 ml) whiskey (preferably Irish whiskey, blended Scotch, or bourbon)

Combine all the ingredients in a cup, stir well, and enjoy.

Spiked Hot Chocolate

1 packet hot cocoa mix

8 ounces (240 ml) hot water

1 ounce (30 ml) good-quality bourbon, brandy, rum, or aquavit

Combine all the ingredients in a cup, stir well, and enjoy. If you have brought cinnamon for cooking, you can add a pinch for extra complexity.

Spiked Mocha

7 ounces (210 ml) hot coffee or 1 packet instant coffee and 7 ounces (210 ml) hot water

1 packet hot cocoa mix

1 ounce (30 ml) bourbon, brandy, rum, or aquavit

Combine all the ingredients in a cup, stir well, and enjoy.

Spiked Mint Tea

1 tea bag mint tea

1 tablespoon (15 g) brown sugar or honey

1 ounce (30 ml) good-quality bourbon, rum, or aquavit

Steep the tea in 7 ounces (210 ml) hot water for about 5 minutes. Remove the tea bag and stir the brown sugar and your spirit into the hot tea.

Spiked Chamomile Tea

1 tea bag chamomile tea

½ tablespoon (8 g) lemonade powder

½ tablespoon (8 g) granulated or brown sugar

1 ounce (30 ml) good-quality gin, vodka, bourbon, or Scotch

Steep the tea in 7 ounces (210 ml) hot water for about 5 minutes. Remove the tea bag and stir the lemonade powder, sugar, and your spirit into the hot tea. You can also try this toddy with English breakfast tea.

STREAMLINED "OLD FASHIONED"

SPIKED LEMONADE

2 ounces (60 ml) good whiskey

1 teaspoon brown sugar

Splash of water

Orange peel, optional

Combine all the ingredients in a cup. Stir until the sugar dissolves (if you like a sweeter drink, you can use more sugar). If you have an orange or a clementine packed with you, cut off a little round coin of orange peel, squeeze it over your drink, then add it to the cup.

8 ounces (240 ml) lemonade or lemon-flavored electrolyte drink, prepared per package directions

1 ounce (30 ml) good-quality bourbon, gin, tequila, rum, or vodka

Combine all the ingredients in a cup and enjoy. If you have found berries along the trail, crush some in to be extra fancy! Or add a pinch of cayenne, if you have some in your spice kit. You can also prepare your lemonade with hot water to enjoy as a hot toddy.

Chapter Three

CAR CAMPING

AH, THE YIN AND YANG OF CAR CAMPING. YOU GET all the ruggedness of the outdoor life with the horsepower to carry anything you want, the curves and angles of the natural world as a backdrop to the curves and angles of a steel box that can travel at unnatural speeds. F. Scott Fitzgerald once wrote offhandedly that "the test of a first-rate intelligence is the ability to hold two opposed ideas in the mind at the same time." So by this measure, I'm going to say car camping is pretty darn smart! Not to mention the options it opens up for cocktailing.

Whether you're road-tripping across the country or heading to a state park for the weekend, the luxury of car camping means that you can bring a little bar setup to go with your kitchen setup, and you probably won't throw out your back. And crucially, bringing a cooler means you can bring some ice, which expands your cocktail horizons infinitely. (For all the details on ice and camping, check out the ice section in chapter 1.) The key lies in planning. One of the simplest ways of doing this is to choose one favorite spirit to bring, and then assemble the ingredients to make two or three different cocktails with it, plus an easy mixer such as ginger beer or grapefruit soda. For example, with a bottle of rum you can plan to make Campsite Mojitos (page 81) and Chai Blossom Toddies (page 93), and mix the rum with ginger beer for Dark and Stormys. Get packing! The wilderness is calling!

You've Arrived

YOU ROLL INTO YOUR CAMPSITE, STEP OUT,
and shake the stuffiness of the car off of you. As you lift bins
of gear from your trunk and scope out the perfect spot to
pitch your tent, it sounds like a good moment to celebrate
your arrival, doesn't it?

◆

MAKE-AHEAD MARGS

Serves 6

You could read the book How to Win Friends and Influence People, *sure. Or you could just make them margaritas. Cocktails ebb and flow in popularity, but the margarita is like a large rock on the beach, unperturbed by the movement of the tides. No one says no to a good margarita. And when you produce a container of perfect slushy margs to share at your campsite, well, your popularity will be just as assured.*

The trick here is to mix the margarita ingredients and then freeze them for a couple of days before packing them in your cooler. You can also experiment with making other slushy cocktails to bring camping using this technique (such as the Sbagliato Slushy on page 56). To ensure that the cocktail will freeze at all, it is best to clock in at right around 8 to 10 percent alcohol. It also needs to have more of the sweet elements and less of the boozy and tart than a nonfrozen cocktail.

◆

10 ounces (300 ml) blanco tequila

6 ounces (180 ml) freshly squeezed lime juice

4½ ounces (135 ml) Cointreau

4½ ounces (135 ml) simple syrup (see page 11)

6 ounces (180 ml) water

Lime wedges (optional, for serving)

Coarse salt (optional, for serving)

In a pitcher, mix the tequila, lime juice, Cointreau, simple syrup, and water together until well combined. Pour the mixture into a heavy-duty zip-top freezer bag and seal carefully. Place your bagged margarita into another zip-top freezer bag and seal this one as well. The double bagging makes for safer transport. If you prefer, you can use a freezer-safe container.

Freeze for at least 2 days, taking the bag out and gently shaking it a couple of times over the course of the freezing time to make sure all the ingredients are staying incorporated. Because of the alcohol content, it won't be frozen solid but will be more of a thick slushy consistency.

Pack your frozen margarita in the coldest part of your cooler. The margarita will, of course, melt over time, so it is best served your first night in camp. To serve, smush the mixture around to break up any large crystals, then divide the cocktail among 6 cups. If desired, you can rim your cups with coarse salt first by running a lime wedge around each cup edge and then rolling the edge in salt.

SBAGLIATO SLUSHY

Serves 6

Sbagliato is basically Italian for "screwed up." Legend has it that the Negroni Sbagliato came about in Milan when a harried bartender grabbed a bottle of Prosecco instead of gin while mixing a Negroni cocktail. Rather than sending it back, the customer who received the bungled cocktail approved of it and drank it right up. Now, having been behind a bar, in the weeds, with customers lined up six thick, I know how easy it is to make any number of mistakes. My favorite from our bar is when two of our bartenders, side by side, accidentally added carbonated water before shaking the cocktails they were making.

No matter how it may have first come on the scene, a Negroni Sbagliato is one of the most perfect early-evening drinks. Appetite-whettingly bitter but with a sense of playfulness, the Negroni Sbagliato fills the bill when it's 4:45 p.m. and you're not quite ready to start with dinner preparation. Inspired by the rampant popularity of the Negroni Slushy, I thought I would try making a Negroni Sbagliato Slushy. The candy-red color of the slushy teases you into expecting a cherry freeze pop. Then you're hit with waves of complex citrus and herbal flavors and a residual bounce from the frozen Prosecco bubbles. Freeze the cocktail ahead of time and break it out your first night in camp to bring a little Italian trattoria to the woods.

6 ounces (180 ml) sweet vermouth

6 ounces (180 ml) Campari

12 ounces (360 ml) Prosecco

1 can (12 ounces [360 ml]) Italian orange soda

In a pitcher, mix the vermouth, Campari, Prosecco, and soda until they're fully combined, then pour the mixture into a heavy-duty zip-top freezer bag and seal carefully. Place the bag into another zip-top freezer bag and seal this one as well. The double bagging makes for safer transport. If you prefer, you can use a freezer-safe container. Freeze for at least 2 days, taking the bag out and gently sloshing the contents around a couple of times over the course of the freezing time to make sure all the ingredients are staying well mixed. Because of the alcohol content, it won't be frozen solid but more of a thick slushy consistency. Pack the cocktail in the coldest part of your cooler. It will melt as you travel, so it is best served your first night in camp.

SWITCH IT UP! At Cane & Table, in New Orleans, they make a similar frozen cocktail to this with sweet vermouth, Campari, and cola instead of the Prosecco and orange soda. It's a pitch-perfect blend of high-brow and low-brow.

FREEZER MARTINI

Serves 3 or 4

Of all the cocktails, the martini may be the one that relies the most on a deep chill to keep it balanced. An insufficiently cold martini is not worth drinking. Some bars are taking this fact so seriously that when they serve a martini, only a portion of it comes in your glass; the rest arrives in a small container buried in ice for you to replenish your drink as you go.

That might make it seem like bringing a martini camping is ludicrous. But, wait: not only can we put a person on the moon, but humankind can also make bottles that keep things very, very hot or very, very cold for a suspiciously long amount of time. (I once burned my mouth on three-day-old coffee. I'm still in shock.)

This means you can make a batch of martinis, freeze until it's silky and as close to absolute zero as possible, then take advantage of the amazing technology of a vacuum-insulated thermos to transport the drink to your campsite. Once your tent is pitched, you can fish out your thermos, pour yourself a stiff drink, and toast to the worthwhile application of human ingenuity.

2 ounces (60 ml) water

9 ounces (270 ml) dry gin

3 ounces (90 ml) Dolin dry vermouth

3 dashes orange bitters

Special equipment: 16-ounce (480 ml) vacuum-insulated thermos

Put the water in the vaccum-insulated thermos and put it in the freezer without the top on. In a separate, freezer-safe bottle, combine the gin, vermouth, and orange bitters. Seal this one, and put it in the freezer as well. Let both things freeze for at least 24 hours. Before you leave, pour the freezer martini into the thermos with the now-frozen water. Seal the thermos. The martini should stay cold for at least 24 hours, and the ice will slowly melt into it.

SWITCH IT UP! This technique will also work with other all-booze cocktails such as a Negroni or one of my favorites, the Lucien Gaudin (2 parts gin to 1 part each Campari, Cointreau, and dry vermouth). Just use the ratio tips from chapter 2 to calculate the proper volume for your thermos.

MAPLE SYRUP OLD FASHIONED

Serves 1

My husband Joel's grandparents were the stuff of legends. His grandfather was an experimental airplane test engineer who rarely spoke, and his grandmother was a chain-smoking, chain-talking force of nature who was still teaching water aerobics at age ninety. When she was finally stuck living in a nursing home, she started a thriving business making and selling beaded jewelry to all the ladies in the home. In their early retirement, they were masters of car camping, traveling all over the country in a Lincoln Town Car with a closet bar across the back seat to keep their polyester leisure clothes from wrinkling. They had a sleek leather suitcase that held the essentials for their daily Old Fashioned. They really knew how to live.

½ teaspoon maple syrup, or more to taste

2 dashes Angostura bitters

2 ounces (60 ml) rye whiskey or bourbon

Orange-peel coin, for garnish

Stir the maple syrup, bitters, and whiskey together in your cup. Taste and add another ½ teaspoon of syrup if desired. Squeeze the orange-peel coin, peel side facing down, over the cocktail to spritz orange oil over the cocktail. Add a piece or two of ice to your cocktail, give another stir, and enjoy.

Morning Tipples

YOU WAKE TO THE CHATTER OF BIRDS, THEN lift the flap of your tent to the morning sun, pouring like honey through the doorway. The vast expanse of a day with no commitments spreads gloriously before you. As you start to bustle about with your breakfast ingredients and other heads poke cheerfully out of other tents, you just might find yourself thinking, "I feel like having something a little more than just coffee on this special morning."

BLOODY MARY

Serves 4

I must begin with a confession. I don't like Bloody Marys. I know; it's amazing I have any friends. At least where I live in the upper Midwest, Bloody Mary affection verges on worship. It's a sancti-fied Sunday brunch ritual, accompanied by a meal's worth of garnishes and a small glass of beer called a "snit." But, in spite of many good-natured "I'll-have-a-gos," I still don't like the drink. If I get within a 10-foot radius of a Bloody Mary, I find myself thinking, "Take out the alcohol, heat the drink up, and serve it to me as soup. Please. And add a grilled cheese. Thanks." I guess I resent the Bloody Mary for what it's not.

However, if on a Sunday morning you decide to forgo a hike in favor of lazily nudging bacon about in a cast-iron pan over a fire, I won't begrudge you your Bloody Mary. In fact, I've asked our head bartenders to share the perfect recipe and they delivered—complete with a delicious skewered garnish.

FOR THE SKEWERS

4 green olives

4 cubes cheddar cheese

4 cubes hard salami

4 Peppadew peppers or banana peppers

4 long toothpicks

To make the skewers, at home, thread an olive, a cheese cube, a salami cube, and a pepper onto each toothpick. Place these skewers in a zip-top bag or a container for transporting.

recipe continues

HELP! MY FRIENDS ALL LIKE DIFFERENT THINGS IN A BLOODY MARY!

It's true, people have strong and varied opinions about proper balance in their Bloody. One way to accommodate this is not to mix the Bloodies ahead of time. You can bring vegetable (or tomato) juice, plus all the truly necessary ingredients—celery salt, lemon juice, horseradish, hot sauce, and Worcestershire sauce are the nonnegotiables—and let everyone make their own drink in camp. It's a lot of little bottles to pack, but it does make it bloody customizable!

FOR THE DRINKS

32 ounces (960 ml) vegetable juice, chilled

1 tablespoon (20 g) molasses

1 tablespoon (6 g) ground cumin

2 tablespoons (30 g) prepared horseradish

1 ounce (30 ml) Worcestershire sauce

½ ounce (15 ml) hot sauce (such as tabasco)

4 ounces (120 ml) pickle juice (the bartender fave at our distillery is to use pickled beet juice or a combination of beet juice and dill pickle juice)

2 ounces (60 ml) fresh lemon juice

1 teaspoon celery salt

1 teaspoon black pepper

8 ounces (240 ml) vodka

To make the drinks, also at home, in a large pitcher, combine the vegetable juice, molasses, cumin, horseradish, Worcestershire, hot sauce, pickle juice, lemon juice, celery salt, and pepper, tasting and adjusting anything to suit your taste as you go. Pour into a large mason jar, thermos, or water bottle, cover tightly, and refrigerate until you're ready to go. If using a mason jar, pack it snug into a corner of your cooler, wedging it in with other things so that it doesn't get jostled.

At the campsite, divide the vodka among 4 cups, then top each with the Bloody Mary mixture. Add ice, if you like ice in your Bloody, and top each cup with one of the skewers.

SPIKED ARNOLD PALMER

Serves up to 9

As refreshing and summery as a skinny-dip in a mountain lake, and less likely to mortify your kids, the Arnold Palmer is a timeless combination of iced tea and lemonade, popularized by the golfer Arnold Palmer. Sources say Mr. Palmer actually preferred his eponymous drink to be made with 3 parts tea and 1 part lemonade, but most often it is made with equal parts of the two. I say go with whatever floats your boat . . . or sinks your putt. If you have commercially prepared iced tea and lemonade, you can totally make your Arnold Palmer with those. No one's judging here. But if you want a drink with extra zip, make it from scratch. I like to make a tea syrup, rather than iced tea, because I think the final drink tastes less muddy. And it is equally delicious spiked or unspiked.

TEA SYRUP

1 cup (200 g) sugar

1 cup (240 ml) water

3 tea bags of black tea

FOR EACH COCKTAIL

1 ounce (30 ml) Tea Syrup

¾ ounce (23 ml) lemon juice

1½ ounces (45 ml) vodka (gin and bourbon are also yummy choices)

4 ounces (120 ml) water

Lemon wedge, for garnish (optional)

To make the syrup, combine the sugar and water in a pot and bring to a boil, stirring to dissolve the sugar. As soon as the water comes to a gentle boil, remove the pot from the heat and add the tea bags. Steep for 8 minutes, stirring occasionally, then remove the tea bags, gently squeezing any liquid from them into the pot. Set the syrup aside to cool.

To make each cocktail, combine the syrup, lemon juice, vodka, and water in a cup, stir, and add ice. Garnish with a lemon wedge, if you wish.

NOTE: For 9 cocktails you will need a full recipe of Tea Syrup, 6¾ ounces (203 ml) lemon juice, 13½ ounces (405 ml) vodka, and 36 ounces (1,080 ml) water.

GREAT DANE (AN AQUAVIT SALTY DOG)

Serves 1

We pulled up to our friends Kate and Ben's cabin around 9:00 in the morning. Kate was still in bed, but the summer morning sun was already hot as it dappled through the trees and glittered off the lake. As our kids ran straight to the water, Kate hauled herself out of bed to start cinnamon rolls baking in their wood-fired oven, and we fished our one contribution out of the car, a bottle of our aquavit. We hadn't had time to pack much. But, as we mixed it with fresh grapefruit juice and handed cups around, it felt like plenty.

Grapefruit juice, in spite of its bitter edge, is surprisingly friendly with a lot of different spirits. If you use vodka in this drink (and leave off the salt) you'll have a Greyhound. With gin, it's a Salty Dog. Aquavit, a caraway-flavored Scandinavian spirit, makes the drink dance with a tango of sweet and savory, salty and sour. I've dubbed it the Great Dane because not only is Denmark one of the world's largest producers of aquavit, but the Danes are also renowned for their brunches, which can last upwards of seven hours. For this drink, choose an aquavit that has a light, caraway-forward style. Avoid aquavits with dill.

The vanilla salt is not an absolute must, but it is a wonderful ingredient to have in your repertoire. Once you have it, you may find yourself sprinkling vanilla salt into and onto everything. Think: butternut squash soup, roasted halibut, beet and chèvre salad, sautéed apples, chocolate chip cookies, ice cream sundaes . . . It adds an evocative wisp of perfume, like a very old memory that flickers through your mind and is gone again just as soon as it arrived.

Coarse kosher salt
½ vanilla bean
Grapefruit or lime slice
1½ ounces (45 ml) aquavit (or gin)
4 ounces (120 ml) fresh grapefruit juice

Pour about ¼ cup (74 g) of salt into a small bowl. Split the vanilla bean in half and scrape the seed paste out into the salt. Rub the vanilla into the salt until the little black flecks are evenly distributed.

Run the slice of grapefruit or lime around the rim of your glass, then roll the glass rim in the salt to coat it. Add the aquavit (or gin), grapefruit juice, and a few ice cubes to your glass.

BMB (BLUEBERRY MAPLE BOURBON)

Serves 1

If you're car camping and you haven't brought supplies for making pancakes, then you're doing it wrong. Since we're friends, I'm going to give you the benefit of the doubt. I'm also going to give you a tip: simmer some blueberries with maple syrup until you have a lovely, loose, jammy blueberry syrup. Use this syrup for your pancakes, but first, spirit away a few spoonfuls of the blueberry-maple liquid for this bramble-like brunch (or anytime) cocktail. I like to throw a little soda water on top of the cocktail for a light fizz, but it's perfectly delicious without it if you haven't brought soda water with you.

BLUEBERRY MAPLE SYRUP

1 cup (150 g) fresh blueberries

½ cup (120 ml) maple syrup

1 tablespoon (15 ml) water

FOR EACH COCKTAIL

1½ ounces (45 ml) bourbon

1 ounce (30 ml) Blueberry Maple Syrup

½ ounce (15 ml) lemon juice

2 ounces (60 ml) soda water (optional)

To make the syrup, combine the blueberries, maple syrup, and water in a small pot and bring to a boil over your camp stove, then immediately turn down to a very low simmer and simmer gently for about 10 minutes, until the blueberries have burst and the sauce has just barely started to thicken. Set aside to cool until you're ready to use. For each cocktail you're making, gently spoon off 1 ounce (30 ml) of the liquid, leaving the berries behind if possible. Use the remaining maple blueberry mixture as a pancake topping.

To make each cocktail, shake the bourbon, syrup, and lemon juice with a handful of ice until chilled. Dump the cocktail, ice and all (fun fact: in bartender lingo, this is called "dirty ice"), into your cup. Top with soda water, if using.

Hammock Happy Hour

IT'S 5 O'CLOCK SOMEWHERE, BUT WHO

even has a watch on?! It's time to sip on something that
tastes as carefree as you feel as you settle into a hammock
with a good book or pull out a pack of cards for a game
with friends.

WISCO-STYLE BLOOD AND SAND

Serves 1

I may get in trouble for calling this a Blood and Sand at all. The Blood and Sand is a classic cocktail, named after a bullfighting movie, interestingly. And though classic, it's a little odd. A combination of Scotch, sweet vermouth, orange juice, and a cherry liqueur called Cherry Heering, the flavors can be . . polarizing. Well then, I thought, what's so wrong with polarizing the situation a little more? I've made the Blood and Sand a bit more camping friendly by taking a cue from the playbook of the Wisconsin Old Fashioned. (Another polarizing cocktail! Is nothing sacred?!). The Wisco-Fashioned is not a real Old Fashioned. Our friends in Wisconsin muddy the cocktail waters by muddling cherries and orange slices with brandy instead of whiskey. They even go so far as to top the cocktail with soda. I won't do that to you, but I do think that using orange slices and cherries instead of orange juice and cherry brandy—skip the soda—makes for a pleasant version of the Blood and Sand, even if it is unorthodox.

The cherries I recommend for this are the Amarena cherries made by Fabbri. Not only are they delicious, but they can also be purchased in stout little jars that are convenient for tucking into the corner of a backpack or cooler for traveling.

2 cocktail cherries

½ small orange, cut into quarters, peel left on

½ ounce (15 ml) sweet vermouth

1½ ounces (45 ml) blended Scotch

In your shaker or water bottle, muddle the cherries and orange slices. Add the vermouth and Scotch plus a handful of ice cubes. Close the shaker and shake as hard as you can for 10 seconds like, really go ballistic. Strain into your cup and serve. Unless you brought a fine-mesh strainer, there will be some little fruit chunks in there. Think of them like tasty confetti.

HOW TO SQUEEZE CITRUS BY HAND

If you're making a lot of cocktails, chances are you'll find yourself squeezing a lot of citrus. It's always worth using freshly squeezed citrus. The flavor is infinitely superior, and citrus fruit, though bulky, doesn't bruise easily, making it good for transport. If you're not hurting for space or weight, you might want to bring a handheld citrus press to help with your squeezing. But you definitely don't need one because squeezing citrus by hand is easy and oftentimes even more effective than using a press. (I once squeezed 75 limes, 125 lemons, and 60 grapefruits by hand for a wedding in north Idaho, so I had a lot of time to think about this.) It will also make you acutely aware of any tiny cuts on your hands that you didn't realize you had!

To squeeze a lemon, a lime, or an orange by hand, first take the whole fruit and roll it against a hard surface. This softens it and makes it easier to squeeze. Cut the fruit in half, then cut it into quarters by cutting perpendicular to the direction of the fruit segments. Remove the seeds. Hold the fruit quarter between your thumb and first two fingers, use one or both hands depending on what is most comfortable for you, and squeeze the juice out. If I'm squeezing a grapefruit by hand, first I grumble because grapefruits are a pain in the rear end, then I cut it in half, palm it like a basketball, and squeeze it that way (you may need to use both hands if you have smaller hands). Grapefruit juice is my one exception to the always fresh rule. Fresh bottled grapefruit juice that is not from concentrate is perfectly acceptable for camping cocktails.

CAMPING SANGRIA

Serves 6

Sangria is my husband's happy hour kryptonite. He can't stop drinking it, and he never remembers to keep track of how many glasses he's had. And it's easy to see why. Sangria is easy to love! It's fun, it's got pizzazz. It's not too sweet, or too serious. It likes long walks on the beach and watching the sunset . . .

The genius move of adding grapefruit in this sangria comes from Madeline Puckette, the sommelier and educator behind the website Wine Folly. Grapefruit is an unusual addition, but it single-handedly adds complexity and fruit without adding too much sweetness. And it means the sangria doesn't have to sit in the refrigerator for hours to absorb fruit flavors. It's ready to drink right away. I love the contrast of strawberries and grapefruit, but you can use any chopped fruit you like. Also, though it doesn't need it, feel free to add ½ cup (120 ml) brandy to your sangria if you're feeling cheeky.

32 ounces (960 ml) full-bodied red wine, suchh as Merlot

8 ounces (240 ml) freshly squeezed grapefruit juice

¼ cup (50 g) sugar

Juice of 1 lime

1 cup (170 g) chopped strawberries

Combine the wine, grapefruit juice, sugar, and lime juice in a bowl, pitcher, or large water bottle and stir until the sugar dissolves. Add some ice and the berries and serve.

ON BOXED WINE

Boxed wine is saddled with a bad reputation, but it's actually a brilliant idea. The vacuum bag inside the box keeps the wine from oxidizing even once it's opened, and the packaging is lightweight and unbreakable, which is a boon for bringing wine on outdoor adventures. Luckily for us, bit by bit more quality wine is becoming available in boxes. If you feel unsure, just talk to the wine buyer at your favorite local liquor store to get recommendations. Also, if you remove the cardboard box, you'll have a very packable squishy-like bag that you can stuff anywhere.

GRILLED ORANGE COBBLER

Serves 1

A cobbler is kind of like a streamlined, single-serve sangria made with any type of wine or forti-fied wine you like. In the late 1800s it was the most popular cocktail in the United States, and I think it's time for a comeback. To paraphrase cocktail historian (and my favorite cocktail writer) David Wondrich, on a warm afternoon, I'd much rather have a cobbler in hand than not. Grilling the orange is not traditional, but it brings out a fire-kissed marmalade flavor and adds an extra layer of depth. A proper cobbler is built with crushed ice—the name cobbler is a reference to the ice, which was thought to look like cobblestones. To make crushed ice, take some of your ice, put it in a bag, and give it a little pounding with a mallet or another heavy object. Small ice cubes will also work just fine. For the wine, you can use red, pink, or white! They all work as long as you use a dry or an off-dry style. With any wine, feel free to adjust the amount of sugar to your taste.

2 round slices of orange

1½ teaspoons (6 g) sugar

6 ounces (180 ml) wine

Fruit for garnish (optional)

While your grill is hot, place the orange slices on the grill. Allow them to cook undisturbed for about 3 minutes, until grill marks have appeared, then flip and grill for about another 3 minutes until the second side is also showing grill marks. Take the orange slices off the grill and set them aside to cool for about 10 minutes.

Put the orange slices in a cup, add the sugar, and gently press the sugar and fruit together to start dissolving the sugar in the juices. Add the wine and a generous scoop of crushed ice or small ice cubes from your cooler. Use a spoon to churn the ingredients and the ice up and down in the glass for about 20 seconds. To make this a true cobbler, you should decorate the heck out of the top of your cup with pieces of fruit before serving. To make it practical, and still tasty, you can drink it without additional fruit garnishes.

CAMPSITE MOJITO

Serves 1

When I was young and foolish, I had a boyfriend who set himself the mission of learning to make a perfect mojito. The Internet was not chock-full of cocktail recipes back then, and he never succeeded. He only ever produced solidly mediocre mojitos. Obviously that relationship was not going anywhere. With this recipe you will never be plagued by mediocre mojitos. It is bright, but not overly acidic, with a wallop of cooling mint. At home I'm vehemently opposed to cocktails with stuff in them—strain that shit out!—but camping calls for exceptions to this rule because, let's be serious, who is really going to double strain their camp cocktail? As such, cocktails like the mojito are good camp companions because you're actually supposed to leave the shaken herbs in the finished cocktail.

Fresh herbs are light and easy to pack with you when camping. To pack them so they stay the freshest, dampen a couple layers of paper towels with water, then loosely roll the herbs in the damp (not wet) paper towels, and seal the bundle in a perforated plastic bag or a plastic bag that has had some holes punched into it for air circulation. In your cooler, soft herbs such as mint, basil, and cilantro should stay good for 3 to 5 days. Sturdier herbs such as thyme and rosemary will keep for a couple of weeks.

6 medium-size fresh mint leaves, plus a sprig for garnish

1 tablespoon (13 g) sugar

½ ounce (15 ml) water

1 ounce (30 ml) fresh lime juice

2 ounces (60 ml) white rum with crisp, light flavors (my go-to is Flor de Caña)

In a shaker or water bottle, gently muddle the 6 mint leaves. Add the sugar, water, and lime juice, and stir or swirl until the sugar starts to dissolve. Add the rum and about ¾ cup (150g) of small ice cubes. Shake vigorously, but briefly, just 10 seconds, then dump the cocktail, ice and all, into your cup. Garnish with a mint sprig. Settle into a hammock and let your cares drift away.

CHANGE IT UP! You can riff off of the mojito by swapping in different herbs and spirits. Try using basil leaves instead of mint and gin instead of rum. Or use a couple of sprigs of thyme with lemon juice and vodka instead of lime and rum.

MIXING WITH BEER

It's Friday after work, and you've decided to throw your gear in the back of your car and get out of dodge. The impulse is to toss in a six-pack and hit the road. Go ahead and follow your impulse, but make your beer do double duty, using it for mixed drinks as well.

Now, I've led entire conference sessions on beer cocktails, and I've wiggled beer into everything from a Manhattan riff to a julep variation. But by far my favorite thing to make with beer is the delightful family of drinks known as radlers. And not just because they remind me of being twenty and traipsing through the Black Forest, I swear.

The radler, a combination of beer with fruit soda or lemonade, was dreamed up in Germany in the early 1900s as a refreshing drink for parched cyclists. If you're wondering what the difference between a radler and a shandy is, well, there isn't much of one. Radler is the German term and shandy is the British one (though shandies began as a beer and ginger ale combination and gradually wandered their way into the beer and lemonade camp from there). Light and thirst quenching, radlers are perfectly suited to spritz o'clock. Many people make their radlers (and shandies) with equal parts beer and fruit juice, but I like them in varying proportions based on the fruit juice I'm using. You can experiment to discover your own favorites, but here are three of mine.

Strawberry Lemonade Radler

Serves 1

3 fresh strawberries

2 tablespoons (25 g) sugar

1½ ounces (45 ml) lemon juice

2 ounces (60 ml) soda water

8 ounces (240 ml) German wheat beer, chilled

In a large cup, vigorously smash the strawberries and sugar together. You can use a muddler or a sturdy wooden spoon, but we're not muddling here; we are attempting to blend the strawberries into as much of a purée as possible by hand. Once you have a berry sauce, stir in the lemon juice and soda water. Top with the beer.

TROPICAL RADLER

Serves 1

3 ounces (90 ml) pineapple juice

8 ounces (240 ml) citrusy India pale ale (IPA), chilled

Add the pineapple juice to a cup, pour the beer over, and enjoy!

BEERMOSA

Serves 1

6 ounces (180 ml) fresh orange juice

6 ounces (180 ml) Belgian wheat beer, chilled

Orange wedge, for garnish (optional)

Add the orange juice to a cup and pour the beer over it. Garnish with an orange wedge, if desired.

CANNED COCKTAILS

It's not just beer that's available in cans these days. Clever distillers (like yours truly, haha) have started to make canned cocktails in an increasingly diverse array of flavors and can sizes. It's a way to have a perfectly balanced cocktail with the ease of cracking open a beer, so what's not to love? Look for canned cocktails made with high-quality ingredients, just as you would use if making a cocktail yourself.

WORKHORSE INGREDIENTS

You know that game we all play when we're little, trying to determine whether a food we love tastes good with absolutely everything? (Yes, bacon would taste *fine* with bubble gum and pickles, okay?!) Well, for cocktail mixing, there are a couple of ingredients that come awfully close to tasting good with absolutely everything and are great to toss into your cooler as an extra mixer for whatever spirits you've chosen to bring along.

GINGER BEER: Most widely recognized for its role in the Moscow Mule (ginger beer and vodka) and the Dark and Stormy (ginger beer and rum), ginger beer is also delicious with gin, whiskey, tequila, and aquavit. The whole family of cocktails that come from mixing a spirit and ginger beer are known as bucks. Just don't forget to squeeze in some lime.

SPEAKING OF LIME, ALMOST ANY SPIRIT TASTES GOOD WITH SUGAR AND LIME: Mix equal parts sugar and lime juice together until the sugar dissolves to make a quick lime cordial (or you can cheat and use lime-ade concentrate) and shake this and some ice with vodka, gin, rum, tequila, mezcal, Scotch, aquavit . . . you name it.

FINALLY, GRAPEFRUIT SODA: Grapefruit soda and tequila with lime makes a well-known cocktail called a Paloma. But don't limit yourself to tequila. Grapefruit soda and lime with whiskey make one of our favorite no-brain-power-necessary cocktails, and the other usual suspects (gin, vodka, etc., etc.) are good too.

Quickie Gin and Tonic

My husband read this chapter over my shoulder and exclaimed, "There's no gin and tonic recipe?!" It's true, there isn't. But do you really need a gin and tonic recipe? I don't think you do. Just mix your favorite gin and favorite tonic, and then squeeze in a lime or lemon wedge. The choice is up to you.

By the Campfire

IF I COULD, I WOULD SPEND EVERY EVENING sitting by a fire with a cozy mug of something snugged into my hand. As you watch the hypnotic dance of flames, you feel connected to humans throughout the ages, all of whom have paused at some time to contemplate the same dance.

PENICILLIN TODDY

Serves 1

The Penicillin cocktail is a modern cocktail with the self-assured air of a classic. The original is shaken and served over ice, but the combination of ginger, honey, and lemon juice fairly screams hot toddy. The grain, spice, and smoke notes from the two types of Scotch settle in comfortably alongside the other flavors, like a cat curling snugly into the edge of a well-loved couch.

Two 1-inch (2.5 cm) rounds of ginger, about ¼ inch (6 mm) thick

¾ ounce (23 ml) honey

¾ ounce (23 ml) lemon juice

4 ounces (120 ml) boiling hot water

2 ounces (60 ml) blended Scotch (Famous Grouse, for example)

1 teaspoon Laphroaig 10-year Scotch

In a mug, combine the ginger slices, honey, and lemon juice, and muddle the ginger to press out some of the ginger juice. Pour the boiling hot water into the mug. Allow to steep for 5 minutes, then stir in the blended Scotch and the Laphroaig. If desired, you can fish out the pieces of ginger. Or leave them in! It's up to you. I take them out because otherwise I know I'll hit myself in the face with a piece of ginger and spill hot toddy all down my front. But that's me, not you.

ON MUDDLING

Plenty of cocktails call for muddling ingredients. It's a nice way to quickly add fresh flavors of herbs or fruits to a cocktail. But muddling is widely misunderstood to mean "pound the heck out of an ingredient." Muddling is actually a much gentler, kinder technique. When you muddle, firmly press down on your herb or fruit (or, in the case of the Penicillin, the ginger) to express the juices or aromatic oils from it, but you don't want it to turn into a crime scene. You can use a heavier hand with sturdy ingredients such as rosemary and ginger; however, be extra careful not to shred the herbs to pieces when muddling because this releases bitter chlorophyll.

SALTED HAZELNUT HOT CHOCOLATE

Serves 1

Hazelnut-chocolate spread, such as Nutella, is extremely handy to bring camping. It doesn't need refrigeration; it makes you feel vaguely European; and it's great for dipping an apple slice, a pretzel, or your finger for an instant treat. Most importantly, you can stir hazelnut-chocolate spread into hot milk to make the most voluptuous hot chocolate you've ever encountered—an overstuffed cashmere pillow for your mouth, if you will. A decent pinch of salt and the thrumming heat of a shot of bourbon ward off the danger of being cloying. One of these by the campfire as a nightcap and you'll float away on a cloud of the sweetest dreams.

8 ounces (240 ml) milk

3 tablespoons (45 g) hazelnut chocolate spread

Generous pinch of salt

1½ ounces (45 ml) bourbon

Marshmallows or whipped cream, for topping (optional)

In a small pot, heat the milk until it's steaming, but not boiling. Add the hazelnut chocolate spread and salt to a mug. Add ½ to 1 ounce (15 to 30 ml) of your milk and whisk it with the hazelnut chocolate spread to thin the spread into a syrup. Stir in the rest of the hot milk. Add the bourbon. Top with marshmallows or whipped cream from a can if you want to get crazy. Which you totally do.

MAKE IT BARTENDER-Y

To take your boozy hot chocolate to the next level, try adding a splash of amaro instead of bourbon. The chocolate-mint notes of Amaro Nardini in hot chocolate are downright magical. The candied orange flavor of Amaro Nonino is also a great fit.

Marshmallow Shot Glass

In the realm of usefulness, I'd classify being able to make a marshmallow shot glass as approximately on par with being double-jointed. By no means is it a necessary skill set, but it sure is fun to break out at parties! And, if you're not careful, someone is liable to get hurt. With great power comes great responsibility, as they say . . .

Toast a marshmallow—regular and jumbo size can both work, but I think regular taste better—over your campfire until it is deeply golden brown all over. Be careful about two things: first, make sure you don't stick your stick the whole way through the marshmallow because a marshmallow straw cannot hold liquid, and

second, do not set your marshmallow on fire. Gently scoot your marshmallow off of the roasting stick and onto a plate, then set it aside to cool completely.

Make a s'more while you wait. As the marshmallow cools, the center should cave in like a molten sugar crater. Fill the crater of your cooled marshmallow with the booze of your choice—I recommend something bracing, such as Fernet Branca—and shoot it quick before the marshmallow dissolves. Chase your shot by indecorously shoving the marshmallow in your mouth. You're welcome.

CHAI BLOSSOM TODDY

Serves 1

Before there was the cocktail, or at least before there was the term cocktail, *there were a number of different spirituous drinks that we now think of as cocktails already in circulation, including punch, slings, juleps, and toddies. Most likely originating in Scotland as a medicinal drink, the toddy—drunk hot or cold!—was an absolute staple of the American beverage scene for the seventeenth and eighteenth centuries. Once a chill creeps into the air, I would say it still is. The most straightforward toddy is simply whiskey with some sweet (usually honey or sugar), some sour (usually lemon), and some spice (a cinnamon stick or a grating of nutmeg). This bare-bones template gives you plenty of leeway to explore spirits and spices, such as this toddy, in which I like to complement the nuanced flavors of chai with an elegant aged rum.*

6 ounces (180 ml) boiling hot water

1 tea bag of chai spiced tea

1½ tablespoons (20 g) brown sugar

½ ounce (15 ml) lime juice

1½ ounces (45 ml) aged Spanish-style rum (I use Plantation Barbados 5 year, for example)

2 dashes Angostura bitters

Combine the hot water and tea bag in a mug and steep for 3 minutes. Taste carefully, and allow the tea to steep a couple more minutes if you like a stronger tea flavor, then remove the tea bag. Stir in the brown sugar (which should dissolve quickly), then the lime juice, rum, and bitters.

MAKE IT BARTENDER-Y

Bartenders love sherry, and so do apples. If you're feeling like a fancy camper, add a generous spoonful of oloroso sherry to your spiked cider. It will add a dry richness to your drink, like the crunch of feet through fallen oak leaves in September. Not to mention, lugging a bottle of sherry with you when you're camping is a clear indication you have your priorities straight. (If you do bring sherry with you, be sure to use some in place of wine in the cobbler recipe on page 78.)

SPIKED CIDER

Serves 6

It's so easy to put on pie-spiced blinders when thinking about apples that we often forget the apple's remarkable affinity for other flavors, such as woodsy green herbs. This deeply aromatic cider plays up apple's savory side with rosemary and bay leaf. Peppery rye is a perfect fit for making it boozy, though I also love this cider in its nonalcoholic form.

One 3- to 4-inch (7.5 to 10 cm) sprig rosemary

1 cinnamon stick

1 bay leaf

8 black peppercorns

Two 2-inch (5 cm)-long strips orange zest, peeled using a vegetable peeler

32 ounces (960 ml) fresh pressed apple cider (not juice)

6 ounces (180 ml) rye whiskey

At home, pack the rosemary, cinnamon, bay leaf, peppercorns, and orange strips in a small zip-top bag or container for transport.

At your campsite, combine the cider with the herbs and spices in a pot over a camp stove, and heat gently until steaming but not bubbling. Allow to cook for 15 to 20 minutes. Remove the cider from the heat and stir in the whiskey. Ladle into mugs to serve.

Chapter Four

THE CABIN

A **CABIN IS A SPECIAL PLACE. PERHAPS THE MOST** special place. We pour the hearts and souls of our families into them, make memories in them, pass them down between generations. The cabin is a place where we find quieter moments, connect with nature and with each other, but still have the affirming coziness of a roof over our heads. Perhaps you call it the cottage or lake house. The sentiment and the purpose are the same.

The cabin is where you'll head for a cocktail on the dock, or a tipple as an accompaniment to a rousing game of Yahtzee. You may keep your cabin drinks simple, but you could also venture into the realm of more complex concoctions because when you're out here, you have the time. Nothing is rushed, everything savored.

Building a cabin bar is as personal as building your home bar, just a bit more streamlined. Or not! I know plenty of people whose cabin bars are way better stocked than their home bars. When beginning to stock a bar, I always advise people to choose one or two cocktails—or perhaps one cocktail for each season—that they love and want to master. Make those your signature cocktails, and stock the ingredients for those. If you start to get really into it, you can always build from there.

On the Dock

DABBLE YOUR TOES IN THE WATER. SUN
yourself as you watch a sailboat go by. Clamber into the
paddleboat to take your turn circumnavigating the floating
dock. Just don't spill your drink.

CHANGE IT UP! As summer's golden sun gives way to autumn's golden leaves and the days are still warm but the nights have a chill, I like to make a variation of this spritz that I jokingly call an Apple-rol Spritz. Just use a dry hard apple cider in place of the Prosecco and soda water, and you can have one too.

APEROL SPRITZ

Serves 1

The one, the only, the iconic spritz. With an Aperol Spritz in hand, relaxation cannot fail to be complete. (Pictured at left).

2 ounces (60 ml) Aperol

3 ounces (90 ml) dry Prosecco

1 ounce (30 ml) soda water

Add the Aperol to a wine goblet half filled with ice. Top with the Prosecco and soda water, stir gently, and serve.

SOMMER SPRITZ

Serves 1

This spritz is an homage to my family's languid days of sunning ourselves, lizard-like, on the rocks at our cabin in Norway. Besides Nordic skiing, sunbathing on the rocks is Norway's national pastime. During the day, coffee keeps you company, but as late afternoon rolls around you can switch out the coffee for a Campari aperitif. This variation is what you find sitting in the center overlap if you draw a Venn diagram of a Bicicletta, a mimosa, and a Garibaldi (sometimes known simply as a Campari-orange). Sweet, bitter, citrusy, effervescent perfection.

2 ounces (60 ml) orange juice

1 ounce (30 ml) Campari

3 ounces (90 ml) dry Prosecco

Add the orange juice and Campari to a wine goblet half filled with ice. Top with the Prosecco, stir gently, and serve.

NARDINI SPRITZ

Serves 1

By replacing Aperol with moodier, darker amaro, you can make your spritz cool-weather ready. I make spritzes with Cynar, Amaro Nonino, and Amaro Montenegro, but my current favorite is this rendition. Inspired by a drink from the restaurant-bar Essex, in Seattle, this spritz tastes as if an Andes Mint wandered off and got lost in the Italian Alps, only to stumble upon a mountain cabin, where the friendly proprietress handed it a glass of Prosecco for refreshment and the revival of good spirits.

¾ ounce (23 ml) Amaro Nardini

4 ounces (120 ml) dry Prosecco

Small coin-shaped piece of lemon peel

Add 2 cubes of ice to a wineglass. Add the amaro and top with the Prosecco. Squeeze the lemon peel over the top of the cocktail to express the lemon oil into it, then discard the peel.

PINEAPPLE-JALAPEÑO MEZCALITA

Serves 1

A cabin is an escape. But sometimes you need to take your escapism to the next level. So go tropical! Pineapple-jalapeño is trendy, but is swiftly becoming classic. The combination is that good. This crowd-pleaser has just the right combination of heat, aroma, and fruit to make you appreciate whatever latitude you're at.

2 ounces (60 ml) mezcal

1½ ounces (45 ml) pineapple juice

½ ounce (15 ml) lime juice

½ ounce (15 ml) simple syrup (see page 11)

1 slice of pineapple or 2 slices of jalapeño, for garnish (optional)

Add the mezcal, pineapple juice, lime juice, and simple syrup to an ice-filled shaker. Shake hard until chilled, then strain into an ice-filled glass. Feel free to garnish with a slice of pineapple if you're feeling fancy, or a slice of jalapeño if you're feeling spicy.

NOTE: If you don't like the smoky flavor of mezcal, feel free to use tequila instead.

DARK RUM DAIQUIRI

Serves 1

A true daiquiri, normally made super dry and light with white rum, is a perfect swim-up-bar drink. If you swap in a dark rum and jiggle the ratio to make it a little sweeter, it is no longer a true daiquiri, but it does become the perfect cabin dock cocktail instead. It's just the right balance between deep flavor and carefree attitude to fuel a jump into refreshing lake water.

2 ounces (60 ml) aged Spanish-style rum

¾ ounce (23 ml) simple syrup (see page 11)

¾ ounce (23 ml) fresh lime juice

A squeezed-out lime half (i.e., the hull of half of a lime that you squeezed to make the juice)

Combine all of the ingredients in a cocktail shaker and add enough ice to fill the shaker two-thirds full. Shake until chilled and strain into a cocktail glass.

CHANGE IT UP! This is the formula I use to make a gin gimlet if I don't have any homemade lime cordial on hand. Just use your favorite gin instead of the rum.

CHILLING IN AN ADIRONDACK

LAKE SUPERIOR IS THE LARGEST OF THE GREAT
Lakes, and in fact the largest body of fresh water in the world. It has accordingly temperamental weather. Long periods of the winter are below zero and blanketed with feet of snow. Spring, if you can call it spring, doesn't start until June and is mainly mud and fog. But in August there may be no place in the world that is more magnificent. The weather is in the mid-70s with breezes like a finger lovingly stroking your cheek. The lake sparkles as if spray-painted with diamonds. And the best possible thing to do is sink into a low chair, holding a cocktail almost as beautiful as the scene, and sit and sit and sit.

PONTOON LIFE

Serves 1

My parents have a small cabin right on the edge of Minnesota's astounding Boundary Waters Canoe Area Wilderness. It is so close to the Boundary Waters that there are strict rules on the types of boats allowed on the lake. Canoes are all right, of course, and so are kayaks, pontoons, and boats with tiny engines that we call put-put boats. We have only a canoe, but my parents' neighbors to the right have a pontoon. Sometimes on a quiet afternoon (well, technically they're all quiet afternoons when you're at the lake), they'll take us for a ride. This is a perfect cocktail to bring on a pontoon outing, preferably in an ugly insulated cabin mug for authenticity. Bourbon and Nonino are splendid together, beautifully rich against the sharpness of lemon. The drink has both heft and freshness, like a pontoon puttering across a dark northern Minnesota lake.

2 ounces (60 ml) bourbon

1 ounce (30 ml) Amaro Nonino

½ ounce (15 ml) lemon juice

½ ounce (15 ml) simple syrup (see page 11)

1 brandied cocktail cherry, for garnish

Combine all the ingredients, except the cherry, in a cocktail shaker. Add ice to fill the shaker two-thirds full, shake hard until well chilled and frothy, then strain into an ice-filled glass. Garnish with the cherry.

GIRL FROM THE NORTH COUNTRY

SERVES 1

My friends and I played Bob Dylan's beautiful ode "Girl from the North Country" as our anthem when we were homesick, after we had left the area to head to school and jobs all over the country. Bob Dylan grew up in the same town as us, so to us the words felt personal. Many years later, after I returned home to the North Country, I crafted this cocktail as an homage to the song, those memories, and northern places. It's pink, but it's strong and not overly sweet, like many gals I know and love.

1½ ounces (45 ml) dry gin

½ ounce (15 ml) pear brandy

½ ounce (15 ml) fresh lemon juice

½ ounce (15 ml) lingonberry syrup or raspberry syrup, made per the recipe on page 159

1 slice of pear, for garnish (optional)

Shake the gin, brandy, lemon juice, and syrup with ice until well chilled. Strain into a cocktail glass. Garnish with a slice of pear, if you wish.

STRAWBERRY FIELDS

ℐERVES 1

Some cabins are set up for solitude, some for hosting happy hour for all the cabins nearby. If you have one of the latter, allow me to let you in on a secret: grilled strawberries. Grilling concentrates the berry flavor and makes them plump and juicy. Lightly grill skewers of strawberries and set some out with whipped chèvre, honey, and grilled bread. Then use some to make this floral, berry twist on a margarita. Your cabin neighbors will thank you.

1 grilled strawberry

2 ounces (60 ml) silver tequila

¾ ounce (23 ml) fresh lime juice

½ ounce (15 ml) St-Germain (or elderflower liqueur made following the method on page 140)

½ ounce (15 ml) simple syrup (see page 11)

To grill strawberries, thread them onto a skewer, place them over a heated grill, and grill over medium-low heat until the berries are softening and juicy. This will take anywhere from 2 to 10 minutes per side, depending on how low your coals are. Allow to cool before using in a cocktail. (Grilled strawberries when hot are amazing on top of cold vanilla ice cream, though.)

To make the cocktail, gently muddle one grilled strawberry in a shaker. Add the tequila, lime juice, St-Germain, and simple syrup, fill the shaker two-thirds full with ice, seal, and shake until chilled. Double strain into a cocktail glass.

GRILLED PEACH BOURBON SMASH

Serves 1

Eating at my husband's family's cabin centers around the grill. So do a number of debates. How charred should grilled food be (or not be)? Do you oil the pizza dough before throwing it on the grill? Why does Uncle Ryan take so interminably long to grill chicken? Eating ribs, however, is never up for debate. Two racks of ribs are the crowning culinary experience of every summer. This grilled peach smash is the perfect accompaniment. Grilling the peaches brings out their sweetness and concentrates their flavor, while just a hint of char pairs beautifully with any barbecue.

½ grilled peach

½ ounce (15 ml) fresh lemon juice

½ ounce (15 ml) maple syrup

2 ounces (60 ml) bourbon

Splash of soda water or ginger beer

To grill peaches, cut them in half and place them, cut side down, on an already hot grill. Cook, undisturbed, until grill marks start to appear (4 to 5 minutes), then flip and cook for 4 minutes on the second side. Allow to cool before using in a cocktail.

To make the cocktail, in a shaker, muddle the peach. Add the lemon juice, maple syrup, and bourbon, then add enough ice to fill the shaker two-thirds full. Shake until well chilled. Double strain into a double rocks glass filled with ice and top with a splash of soda water or ginger beer.

NOTE: Like any cocktail with a lot of soft muddled fruit, this drink is a little slow to strain because the fruit has a tendency to clog up the strainer. If you don't mind fruit chunks in your cocktail, you can just strain through your cocktail strainer and not worry about double straining. Or you can even drink the cocktail with all the fruit in there. You do you!

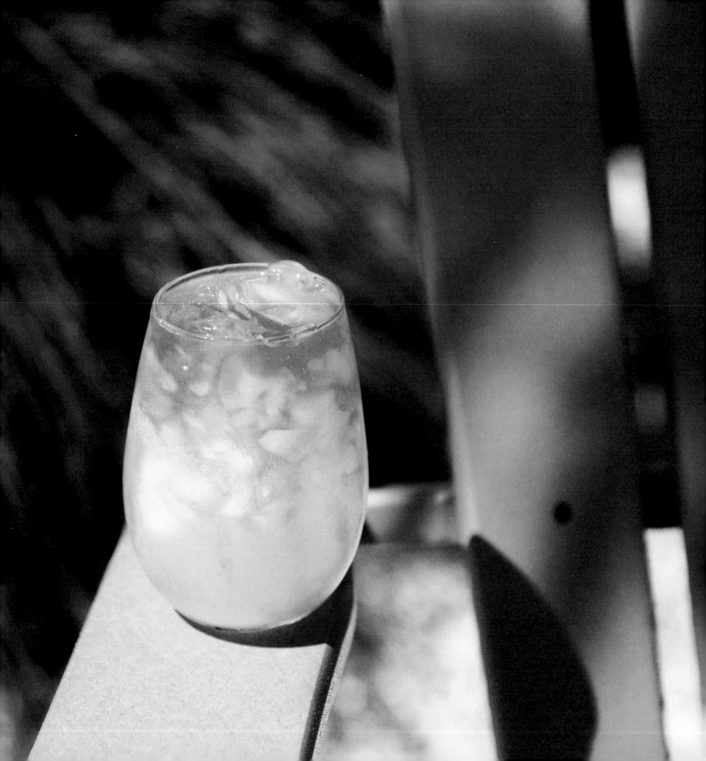

BRAMBLE

Serves 1

Summer in a glass. The cool bite of gin is a perfect foil to jammy berries, so nothing is too sweet nor is it too strong. And it's so pretty! The traditional recipe calls for blackberry liqueur, but gin has such an affinity for berries that I have found you can use any berry syrup or liqueur that you like and it will be delightful. The crushed ice is important for diluting the drink properly, and it's easy to make your own crushed ice by folding ice cubes into a clean dishtowel and whacking them with a mallet, rolling pin, or other heavy utensil—I have used everything from a jar of salsa to a bottle of wine. If you use regular ice cubes instead of crushed, you'll want to add a nice splash of water or soda water.

2 ounces (60 ml) dry gin

¾ ounce (23 ml) fresh lemon juice

½ ounce (15 ml) simple syrup (see page 11)

½ ounce (15 ml) berry syrup, made per the recipe on page 159

Fill a double rocks glass half full with crushed ice. Add the gin, lemon juice, and simple syrup, and stir for about 5 seconds to combine and chill. Fill the glass the remainder of the way with more crushed ice, then drizzle the berry syrup over the top. I leave the choice of whether to stir everything together or enjoy your drink in layers up to you.

STARGAZING

IN THE DARKNESS OF A SKY UNCLOUDED BY
city lights, the stars look thick enough to be a blanket. The
vastness of the sky is gorgeously overwhelming . . . I think
it's time for a nightcap.

MARSHMALLOW MULE

Serves 1

If I'm perfectly honest, this wasn't originally a cabin cocktail. It was a joke cocktail. After years of saying we weren't going to make a vodka at our distillery, we finally buckled under the sheer weight of all the requests we got from eager vodka enthusiasts, and we started to distill one. We hosted a vodka release party, which we called "Not a Vodka Party," on April Fools' Day with artisanal takes on a handful of well-known vodka drinks. The Marshmallow Mule was one of the party drinks, and people loved it so much that they still request it, years later.

Making the marshmallow and ginger syrup does take a little doing, but it doesn't require any fancy equipment or even fancy ingredients. And it's a nice thing to do as an activity during the evening anyway. The toasted marshmallows melted into the syrup give it a dark richness while loads of fresh ginger give it a kick.

MARSHMALLOW AND GINGER SYRUP

10 marshmallows

1 cup (200 g) sugar

1 cup (240 ml) water

½ cup (65 g) grated fresh ginger

FOR EACH COCKTAIL

1½ ounces (45 ml) vodka (or whiskey or rum)

1½ ounces (45 ml) Marshmallow and Ginger Syrup

Soda water

Lime wedges

1 marshmallow, for garnish

To make the syrup, toast the marshmallows over dying embers until they are dark brown and melted inside. Put them into a heavy-bottomed pot and add the sugar and water. Slowly bring to a boil, stirring frequently to dissolve the sugar and the marshmallows. Once you reach a gentle boil, turn the heat down to a simmer and continue cooking and stirring until the marshmallows have dissolved. Remove the syrup from the heat, stir in the ginger, and transfer to a heatproof container. Cover and allow to cool overnight. The next day, strain the syrup through a fine-mesh strainer lined with cheesecloth. The syrup will keep in a tightly sealed container in the fridge for at least 2 weeks.

To make the cocktail, in a tall glass filled with ice, add the vodka and syrup. Top with soda water and gently stir. Squeeze in lime wedges to taste. Stick your garnish marshmallow onto a long toothpick. Light it on fire, blow it out, then stick the toothpick into the cocktail, marshmallow side out of the drink, to garnish.

MALTED WHITE RUSSIAN

Serves 1

I was an extremely tame teenager. My idea of a wild summer night consisted of biking with a gaggle of friends to the local malt shop down along the lakeshore, ordering a hot fudge malt with coffee syrup, and downing the whole thing. My friends and I would sip malts, dig our toes into the smooth pebbled beach, talk about the usual dramatic nothingness that occupies teenage minds, and feel blissfully free.

I don't know whether I love malt because of those ice cream–fueled evenings or because I've always had an innate fondness for the flavor. Either way, I adore malt to this day. Adding a scoop of malted milk powder to a White Russian recreates some of the feel of a malt shop treat, with the added fun of a kick of booze that I hadn't yet discovered in those days. It sends me right back to nostalgic summer nights and the feeling of summer evenings expansive enough to hold all of my dreams.

I use half-and-half instead of the standard heavy cream in a White Russian because I think it makes it more sippable. But heavy cream is, of course, absolutely delicious and takes this drink further toward the realm of the milkshake.

2 ounces (60 ml) vodka

1 ounce (30 ml) coffee liqueur

1 ounce (30 ml) half-and-half

1 tablespoon (8 g) malted milk powder

Add the vodka, coffee liqueur, half-and-half, and malted milk powder to a cocktail shaker. Stir to dissolve the malt. Add ice and shake vigorously until well chilled. Strain into a low glass.

MAKE IT BARTENDER-Y

Instead of vodka, try making your White Russian with aquavit. The heady, almost spicy caraway flavor complements the coffee and malt beautifully. At our bar we call our aquavit version of a White Russian "The Expat."

GLØGG

Serves 6 to 8

Hygge is a Scandinavian term (it's usually said to be Danish, but as a Norwegian I want to get in on some of the credit because we totally use the word as well) for the general concept of making things cozy and enjoying cozy moments with friends and family. The idea has been embraced by everyone from designers to life coaches as a secret to happiness. I can't promise that hygge is the secret to happiness, but I will promise that being intentional about getting cozy is a lovely thing. And sharing steaming mugs of gløgg (the boozy Scandinavian answer to mulled wine) in the winter at the cabin is hygge-er than a bunny wearing cable-knit socks and wrapped up in an eiderdown.

32 ounces (960 ml) full-bodied red wine

5 cloves

2 cardamom pods, cracked

1 stick cinnamon

2 slices fresh ginger, each about ¼ inch (6 mm) thick and 1 inch (2.5 cm) across

½ cup (170 g) honey or (100 g) sugar

8 ounces (240 ml) aquavit or brandy (optional, but oh so recommended)

Raisins, for serving (optional)

Slivered almonds, for serving (optional)

Combine the wine, cloves, cardamom, cinnamon, ginger, honey, and aquavit in a heavy-bottomed pot. Heat over low heat for at least a couple of hours. The key to a good gløgg is to heat and infuse it slowly, never letting it come to a boil (to this end, warming and infusing it in a slow cooker actually works great). To serve, ladle the gløgg into mugs (by the way, gløgg and mug rhyme! So, feel free to make a song about it as you ladle) with raisins and slivered almonds in them, if desired.

NORTHWOODS SIDECAR

Serves 1

I love aquavit. Maybe because I'm Norwegian, and aquavit is the national spirit of the country. But even without the cultural connection, I think the aromatic caraway flavor of aquavit makes for a fantastic and unexpected cocktail base. At our bar, aquavit is our go-to bottle to grab in the early stages of building a new cocktail idea.

Because of its Nordic pedigree, aquavit also has this way of conjuring dark woods, dramatic mountains, and sturdily built wood cabins. For the aquavit newbie, I like to shake up a variation on a Sidecar. The cocktail has a lovely balance of sweet, tart, and herbal. Avoid aquavits with dill in them for this drink.

2 ounces (60 ml) aquavit, preferably aged

¾ ounce (23 ml) Cointreau

¾ ounce (23 ml) fresh lemon juice

¼ ounce (8 ml) simple syrup (see page 11)

Shake all the ingredients in a cocktail shaker with ice until well chilled. Strain into a cocktail glass and serve.

FIRE PUNCH

Serves 10 to 12

Did you know that Charles Dickens, in addition to authoring a couple of little books you may have heard of, also authored a punch recipe? He sent his recipe in a letter to a friend, and it was unearthed by cocktail historian David Wondrich. What excites me about Dickens's recipe, and is sure to excite anyone else present, is that you light it on fire. Seriously, what could be more fun than hanging out by the fire at the cabin with your family and then—poof!—lighting a bowl (well, technically a fire-safe container or Dutch oven) of punch on fire in front of them? The fire has the dual result of lightly caramelizing the sugar in the recipe and burning off some of the alcohol, which turns out not to be a terrible idea once you see how much is in the recipe.

I've riffed on good old Charles's recipe, switching some of the ratios around and adding pineapple juice for a tiki twist. I've kept the fire. Obviously.

3 lemons

½ cup (100 g) granulated or demerara sugar

16 ounces (480 ml) brandy

10 ounces (300 ml) overproof rum

16 ounces (480 ml) strong brewed black tea, cooled

32 ounces (960 ml) pineapple juice

Freshly grated nutmeg, for garnish (optional)

Lemon wheels, for garnish (optional)

NOTE: You can also use just rum or brandy to streamline the recipe, if you want.

Remove the peels, with no white pith, from the lemons using a vegetable peeler. In an enameled Dutch oven or a heatproof bowl, rub the lemon peels into the sugar with your fingertips. Set this aside for 30 to 60 minutes to let the sugar pull the citrus oils out of the lemon peel. Juice the lemons and set the juice aside. Next, stir the brandy and the rum into the sugar and lemon peel mixture. Using a long-handled metal spoon, scoop up a spoonful of the alcohol. Carefully (CAREFULLY!) use a long match or lighter to light the spoonful on fire. Then, gently lower this into the rest of the mixture to start the whole bowl on fire (it may take a minute of holding the spoon of fire just partially submerged to get the rest of the spirits to catch fire). The fire will burn a white-blue, rather than yellow. Sit back and enjoy the heat and glow of your fire for 1 or 2 minutes, then use a pot lid to cover the fire and put it out. Take off the lid and pour in the tea, pineapple juice, and reserved lemon juice. Add some ice and allow to chill for a minute. Garnish with a fresh grating of nutmeg and some lemon wheels, if you wish.

THE BEST IRISH COFFEE

Serves 1

Whether enjoyed as a lazy, late brunch pick-me-up or as a dessert to cap off an evening of cribbage and storytelling, Irish coffee is beautifully ephemeral. There's something in the brief moment where the cool of the cream hits your lips just before the warm, boozy coffee enters the picture. For a perfect Irish coffee, it's all about the details. Use coffee that's toasty hot but not scalding hot and cream that's gently whipped so it slumps rather than peaks. Ever since the fateful time I was surprised and enchanted by being given an espresso that had been pulled over a piece of lemon rind, I've often used a hint of lemon zest as a way to give coffee an extra je ne sais quoi. Now that you do sais quoi, I suggest you try it. Use a vegetable peeler to peel the lemon strip so you have no white pith.

1 tablespoon (13 g) demerara sugar (brown sugar will also work)

2- to 3-inch (5 to 7.5 cm) strip of lemon peel with no white pith

1 ounce (30 ml) heavy cream

½ teaspoon granulated sugar

5 ounces (150 ml) piping hot, but not scalding hot, coffee

1½ ounces (45 ml) Irish whiskey

Combine the demerara sugar and lemon peel in an Irish coffee mug or a regular coffee mug, using a spoon to smash the lemon peel into the sugar a bit. Set this aside for about 5 minutes to let the sugar pull the citrus oils out of the peel. This is a good time to whip your cream! Whip the heavy cream with the granulated sugar until it is thickened but still soft (I shake the cream in a sealed jar until it has thickened). Keep the whipped cream in the refrigerator until you are ready

to use it. Next, pour the coffee into the cup with the lemon peel and demerara, add the Irish whiskey, and stir until the sugar dissolves. Top with the whipped cream and enjoy.

CHAPTER FIVE

FORAGED AND FOUND

FORAGING, WHEN IT COMES DOWN TO IT, IS SIMPLY GOING and getting yourself something to eat. Doing that from a supermarket rather than from the field or forest is actually the newfangled trend. I have been foraging since I was a child, brought up to seek out wild berries, pick wild onions, nibble on wood sorrel, and suck on sumac berries as a treat. So it was a no-brainer to use foraged ingredients for drink making, once I started a distillery and bar. I love the renewed interest in foraging because I think foraging reconnects us with nature and the fact that all of our food, whether we see it or not, relies completely on the land. It's a way to discover and appreciate new flavors, as well as some ingredients that are incredibly nutritious.

Before you start to forage for ingredients from the forest or your backyard, make sure you know what you are doing. Nature isn't joking around. She is abundant, and generous, but she can also kill you. Never eat anything if you aren't 100 percent certain that it is safe. In fact, I am an anxious forager—which I think is the best type of forager—and I only pick and eat foods that I am 150 percent sure are safe. The wild ingredients I've chosen to feature in this chapter are mainly ones that have a wide range, are on the easy side to learn to identify, and don't really have poisonous look-alikes. That said, you still should not go picking wild foods until you have learned to forage properly.

*See page 135 for some tips on foraging safety.

SPRING

HERE IN THE COLD NORTH, SPRING TAUNTS US.

After the long winter, spring flits in and out, here one day and gone
the next, making us wonder whether it will ever actually be warm
again. Even as the days begin to warm, frost comes overnight and
slows the growing season. But some intrepid plants do begin to
appear. Sunny dandelions brighten corners of a field, wild leeks poke
up through the carpet of dead leaves in the forest, and flowering
trees blossom, harbingers of bounty to come.

DANDELIONS

IS THERE ANY FLOWER MORE FRIENDLY THAN A dandelion? Sure, they are weeds, but their powerful will to take root and grow in any lawn and through any crack in the road feels to me like a testament to the power of optimism. The dandelion was actually brought to North America by European settlers to grow for food, wine, and medicine. The flower, leaves, and root are all edible. And because it is non-native and definitively a weed, you don't have to worry about over-harvesting as you do with native wild plants.

I remember making dandelion-flower fritters in fifth grade. The flavor was fine, but I couldn't enjoy the thick, feathery texture of the layered flower petals. I much prefer to use dandelion flowers for infusions, in which they give a surprisingly aromatic flavor that reminds me of lemon balm.

The best way to learn to forage is in person, from an expert. Many areas have groups that you can join, with certified herbalists and certified foragers to learn from. Working alongside people like these, you can learn to safely identify wild plants by learning the multiple characteristics you should look for. Always use several points of identification to ensure you know what a plant is, including the habitat, visual cues from different parts of the plant (what its stem, leaves, flowers, and more look like), feel (rough, hairy, smooth, papery types of characteristics), and smell. Learn the time of year plants grow and companion plants they often grow near, and make sure you carefully learn about any poisonous plants in your area so that you are acutely aware of those as well. Supplement what you learn in person by getting a good field guide to plants in your area. As you learn to forage, you will also learn to protect the plants and ecosystems they live in. To protect rare or endangered species and fragile ecosystems, focus your foraging on plants that are abundant and robust—that is to say, weeds. You can even forage for invasive species. Never pick more than you need. And make sure you know whether you are even allowed to forage in the area where you are. Remember that picking wild plants from National Parks is actually illegal.

That's a lot of cautions, I know. But once you've done the work, learned what you need to learn, and made your first spruce syrup or crab apple bitters, the results will be worth it.

DANDELION HONEY

Makes ¾ cup (240 g)

The warm, complex sweetness of wildflower honey is the perfect foil to the bright dandelion-flower aroma. And making an infusion is as simple as stirring the two ingredients together. Not only is this honey a delicious cocktail ingredient, but it is also tasty in tea.

1 cup (about 100 g) dandelion flowers

¾ cup (255 g) honey

Check the flowers to make sure you remove any little insects or other passengers, then put the flowers in a jar. Cover the flowers with the honey, gently pressing the flowers into the honey to make sure there aren't any large air bubbles. Seal the jar and allow to steep for 2 weeks. (You can steep it even longer for a more pronounced flavor.) If you wish to strain the flowers out of the honey, gently heat the honey to make it more liquid, then strain it through a fine-mesh strainer. Store your honey in a sealed jar at room temperature. Honey keeps forever. (Literally. Several years ago it's said that archaeologists found jars of honey in a tomb from ancient Egypt and it was still good for eating.)

To make honey syrup: Combine 2 parts dandelion-infused honey with 1 part water and stir until dissolved.

COCKTAIL

Make a Bees Knees by adding 2 ounces (60 ml) gin, ¾ ounce (23 ml) fresh lemon juice, and ¾ ounce (23 ml) dandelion-infused honey syrup to an ice-filled shaker. Shake until chilled, then strain into a coupe glass.

DANDELION AND BURDOCK ROOTS

TWO OF THE MOST COMMONLY UNDERFOOT WEEDS across the country are also two of the most useful sources of wild nutrition. Dandelion, whose perky yellow flowers and jagged leaves are familiar to almost everyone, also has an edible root. Dried or fresh, the root can be used to make a tea that helps support the liver and kidneys. Burdock has huge, wavy, heart-shaped leaves growing from a rosette of stems that will remind you of rhubarb. In fall, it grows burrs that will stick to your clothes, hair, and pets and generally make themselves very obnoxious. But they did inspire the invention of Velcro! Anyway, fresh burdock root can be peeled and cooked rather like a parsnip, and dried burdock root can be used in a tea very similar to dandelion. But why make tea when you can make something more spirited?

A FORAGER'S NOTE: Burdock roots are easiest to dig up in spring when the leaves are emerging and still small but can also be dug in fall after the first frost. Look for first-year burdock, which has just a rosette of leaves close to the ground and hasn't shot up a central stem for growing flowers. Similar to burdock, dandelion roots are best foraged in either early spring or late fall. Both plants have deep taproots, so you will need a good spade to dig down and dislodge the root from the ground. To dry the roots, wash them well using a brush to scrub off dirt, cut the root into small pieces, then spread the pieces on a baking sheet. Dry them in a 200°F (100°C) oven or in a dehydrator. Store the dried roots in an airtight container. If fully dried, they will keep practically forever.

DANDELION BURDOCK AMARO

MAKES 3 CUPS (720 ML)

This amaro is inspired by dandelion burdock soda, a popular soft drink in the United Kingdom. The natural bitterness of these roots makes them well suited for drinkable bitters, but with more earthiness than most typical amari.

2 cups (480 ml) vodka

2 teaspoons dried burdock root

2 teaspoons dried dandelion root

2 teaspoons dried ginger root

1/8 teaspoon gentian root

1 star anise

1 teaspoon bitter orange peel

Three 2-inch (5 cm)-long strips of orange peel, removed with a vegetable peeler to avoid the white pith

1 cup (240 ml) simple syrup (see page 11)

Combine the vodka, roots, star anise, and orange peels in a sealed jar. Allow to sit for 2 to 3 weeks, shaking occasionally. Add the simple syrup to the jar, reseal, and allow to steep for an additional week. Strain through a fine-mesh strainer lined with cheesecloth into a clean jar. Seal and store at room temperature.

COCKTAIL

The easiest way to use amaro is in an amaro and cola. Just add a generous splash of your amaro to an ice-filled glass, top up with cola, and add a squeeze of lime.

LILACS

THE MOST INTOXICATING MOMENT OF SPRING IS when the lilac blossoms burst forth like millions of tiny purple trumpets filling the air with the strains of their ethereal aroma. Though not originally wild, lilac trees may crop up in natural areas at the edges of where people live. Many people don't know that lilac blossoms are, in fact, edible. When made into syrup or infused into sugar, they have a deep, floral candied flavor and scent.

LILAC (OR ELDERFLOWER OR VIOLET, ETC.) CORDIAL

MAKES 5 CUPS (1.2 L)

Every spring I make a large batch of Lilac Cordial to use in cocktails and to add to lemonade. This cordial method also works with many of the other more widely known aromatic edible flowers, including elderflowers, hibiscus, violets, roses, and citrus blossoms. (To use more herbal blossoms such as hyssop, angelica, borage, and chickweed, try the Foraged Herb Liqueur on page 164.)

8 to 10 lilac flower bunches

1 lemon, thinly sliced into rounds

4 cups (960 ml) water

2¾ cups (550 g) sugar

1½ teaspoons citric acid (omit this if turning your cordial into liqueur)

Shake the flower bunches gently, and carefully pick through them to brush away any visible dirt or insects. Don't wash the blossoms because you will wash away some of the flavorful nectar. Use scissors or your fingers to carefully remove all the tiny flowers from their stems (the stems add a bitter green note if you get any), taking care to remove the flowers at their very bottom because that is where the nectar is. You should wind up with somewhere in the realm of 5 to 6 cups (about 250 to 300 g) of flowers. Place the flowers in a large heatproof glass or ceramic bowl or jar and add the lemon slices.

Combine the water and sugar in a pot and bring it just to a boil, stirring while heating to fully dissolve the sugar. Stir in the citric acid if you are using it. Pour this hot syrup over the flowers and lemon.

Cover the bowl or jar tightly and allow to steep at room temperature for 24 hours. Give the mixture a gentle stir a couple of times over the course of the 24 hours. Refrigerate the mixture to continue steeping for another 2 or 3 days. (Taste first after 2 days, and then if you would like a little stronger flavor, leave it to steep a third day.)

When it is done steeping, strain the mixture through a fine-mesh strainer lined with cheesecloth. Transfer the cordial to clean bottles or jars and keep refrigerated for up to 2 months. You can discard the spent flowers, or you can spread them out on baking sheets and dry them in a

200°F (100°C) oven to make candied lilac flowers, which are fun to use as an edible garnish (we use them to garnish our Lilac Sour—recipe at right) and taste almost like gummy candy.

To make your cordial into a quick floral liqueur: Add 4 ounces (120 ml) vodka for every 8 ounces (240 ml) cordial you make, then allow it to mellow for 2 weeks in a jar in a dark place before using. I do not like to steep flowers directly in alcohol to make liqueur because the gorgeous floral flavor is quickly elbowed out by strong, stemmy vegetal flavors.

COCKTAIL

Make a Lilac Sour by adding ½ ounce (15 ml) egg white, 2 ounces (60 ml) gin or vodka, ¾ ounce (23 ml) fresh lemon juice, and ¾ ounce (23 ml) Lilac Cordial to a shaker, and shake hard with no ice for about 10 seconds. Then fill the shaker two-thirds full with ice. Close the shaker and shake extremely hard for another 10 seconds. Double strain into a cocktail coupe and serve.

SPRUCE AND FIR TIPS

I **STARTED PICKING SPRUCE TIPS ALMOST A DECADE**
ago because I wanted to pickle them. Their flavor is amazing, intensely
piney, citrusy, and lightly tannic. When we started a distillery, I knew
I had to include spruce tips in one of our gins. So, spruce tip gathering has
become an annual spring tradition. The tips, or buds, of spruce and fir trees
are soft and edible when they emerge. They are a shocking chartreuse
green, and picking them is as simple as pinching off the tips. Look for buds
that are about 1½ inches (3.8 cm) long. As they grow longer, the tips become
more pine flavored but also bitter and tougher. Be sure to harvest only a
portion of a tree's tips, and make sure you pick evenly from around the tree
so that you don't cause the branches to grow all catawampus. You can use
the tips fresh, but they also freeze and defrost well.

SPRUCE (OR FIR) SYRUP

MAKES 1/2 CUPS (360 ML)

You could use spruce tips instead of ramps in the pickle recipe on page 153 to make a Spruce Gibson, but when it comes to cocktail ingredients, my favorite is Spruce Syrup. Use it in a gimlet to augment gin's traditional evergreen flavors with an additional pine wallop.

1 cup (about 100 g) spruce (or fir) tips
1 cup (200 g) sugar
1 cup (240 ml) water

Gently clean the spruce tips of any insects or bits of spiderweb and place in a heatproof bowl or jar. Combine the sugar and water in a small pot and bring to a boil, stirring to dissolve the sugar. Pour the hot syrup over the spruce tips, cover, and steep for at least 24 hours, or 48 hours if you would like a stronger flavor. Strain the syrup through a fine-mesh strainer lined with cheesecloth. The syrup will keep refrigerated in a tightly sealed container for at least 2 weeks. To preserve it for longer, add 1 tablespoon (15 ml) of vodka.

COCKTAIL

Shake 2 ounces (60 ml) gin, ¾ ounce (23 ml) Spruce Syrup, and ¾ ounce (23 ml) fresh lime juice with ice until well chilled. Strain into a cocktail coupe and serve.

RAMPS

RAMPS ARE A TYPE OF WILD LEEK THAT ARE SO ABUNDANT in some of the forests where I grew up that when you walk through the groves in springtime the air smells of onion. They are one of the earliest edible things to emerge in spring and they are rich with the concentrated flavor of onion and garlic. Because of their wonderful flavor, they have become trendy with foodies, and the wild populations of ramps, particularly along the East Coast, have been decimated by over-harvesting. So, if you are lucky enough to stumble across a stand of ramps, be very careful about how much and how you harvest.

Ramps take five years to grow to maturity and reproduce, but they can also grow out runners from their bulbs. So, the very best and most sustainable way to harvest ramps is to take only leaves. Take just one leaf from a plant, leaving the second leaf and the bulb undisturbed. The leaves are fantastic in a stir-fry. But if you love pickled ramps, as I do, you can harvest just a portion of the bulb, leaving the roots behind. Gently and carefully dig around the bulb of a plant, making sure that you leave the roots at the bottom of the bulb in the ground. Use a small sharp knife to slice through the bulb, leaving the bottom third in the ground, undisturbed, and taking the top two-thirds with the stem and leaves. Then gently re-cover the root. If harvesting this way, never take more than 5 percent of the plants from a patch of ramps. In fact, I no longer ever take more than about ten plants total, even from the large stands of ramps we have in my area. They are so potently flavored you only need a little to go a long way.

A FORAGER'S NOTE: Ramps are pretty easy to identify once you know what their broad, smooth green leaves and purple-red stems look like. However, they look very similar to lily of the valley, and lilies of the valley are deadly poisonous. But ramps have a distinctly oniony scent, and lilies of the valley do not.

PICKLED RAMPS

MAKES 3 CUPS (720 ML) PICKLE JUICE

You can use just a few ramps to impart a wild leek essence to a jar of pickling liquid that you can then use for many Gibson Martinis. The pickled ramps themselves are amazing chopped and added to sandwiches, tacos, or salads.

Bulbs and stems of 6 to 10 ramps, gently cleaned and sliced into 1-inch (2.5 cm) chunks

1½ teaspoons pickling spice

2 cups (480 ml) Champagne vinegar

1 cup (200 g) sugar

1 tablespoon (18 g) coarse salt

½ cup (120 ml) water

Put the ramps in a quart (1 L) jar. Place the pickling spice in a tea strainer. Combine the pickling spice, vinegar, sugar, salt, and water in a pot and bring just to a boil. Pour over the ramps, close the jar loosely, and place in the refrigerator. You can keep the ramps in the pickling liquid for up to a month. They will take on more vinegar flavor and become softer and softer over time, and the brine will become more ramp flavored, which is really what we are going for because then you can make the savory take on a martini known as a Gibson.

COCKTAIL

Stir 2 ounces (60 ml) excellent-quality gin, 1 ounce (30 ml) blanc vermouth, and 1 teaspoon pickled ramp juice with ice until extremely well chilled. Strain into a martini glass and serve.

SUMMER

WHEN I WAS A CHILD WE SPENT OUR SUMMERS IN
Norway (my mom is from Oslo). Every day we went for a hike, and
every day I moved at a snail's pace because instead of following the
trail, I followed berry bushes. Once I start picking berries I can't stop.
So, instead of exercising my legs, I exercised my plucking fingers as
the wild strawberries and raspberries stretched on endlessly. And
that, in a nutshell, is what summer is all about.

BERRIES

IALWAYS FEEL LIKE LATE-SUMMER BUSHES HEAVY with wild berries are one of the most convincing signs that there is a natural benevolence in the universe. Depending on where you are, it could be blackberries, raspberries, salmonberries, huckleberries . . . The feeling is the same. The joy that comes from finding a patch of ripe berries gives you a strong sense that nature provides—the plucking and eating, the handfuls and mouthfuls, and still there are more and more berries as you move through the brush. Sure, that sense of abundance will be completely gone come January, but in August, sweet August, life is easy. Eat your fill, crush some berries into your lemonade, sprinkle some on your oatmeal. Then, fill up an empty container and bring some home to preserve the summer's bounty.

WILD BERRY SYRUP

Makes about 3 cups (720 ml)

This simple recipe template works with any berry, and because fresh berries only last for a few days, syrup is a nice way to concentrate and save the ephemeral wild berry flavor for later. You can try it in place of simple syrup in cocktail recipes to give the drink a fruity twist, or use berry syrup plus lemon juice and water to make berry lemonade.

2 cups (300 g) berries (strawberries, raspberries, blackberries, blueberries, Juneberries, salmonberries, boysenberries, huckleberries, Oregon grapes . . .)

1 cup (200 g) sugar

1 cup (240 ml) water

1 tablespoon (15 ml) fresh lemon juice

Combine the berries, sugar, and water in a heavy-bottomed pot. Keep the pot uncovered. Slowly bring to a boil, stirring to dissolve the sugar. Once it has boiled, turn the temperature down to a medium-low simmer and simmer for about 15 minutes, using a wooden spoon to crush the berries as they cook. Remove from the heat and strain through a fine-mesh strainer, pressing gently on the berries to make sure all their juice is released (you can stir the leftover smushed berries into yogurt for a treat). Stir the lemon juice into the syrup and allow to cool. The finished syrup will keep in a sealed container in the refrigerator for at least 2 weeks.

COCKTAIL

Use your Wild Berry Syrup in the Bramble recipe on page 117, or add ¾ ounce (23 ml) of chilled berry syrup to a Champagne glass and top with a dry sparkling wine (such as Champagne, Cava, or Prosecco) for a delightful variation on a Kir Royale.

FORAGED BERRY DRINKING VINEGAR (AKA BERRY SHRUB)

MAKES ABOUT 1 1/2 CUPS (360 ML)

Shrubs are a combination of fruit, sugar, and vinegar. They were common in colonial times as a way of making berry syrups last even longer and have become popular drink ingredients again. They are bold and tart and, as a vinegar lover, I can never get enough of them.

1 cup (150 g) berries
1 cup (200 g) sugar
1 cup (240 ml) red wine vinegar

In a nonreactive bowl (such as glass or ceramic), gently crush the berries with the sugar. Cover the bowl, refrigerate, and allow to sit for 24 hours while the sugar draws the juices out of the berries. After 24 hours, add the vinegar and gently stir. Cover again and refrigerate for another 2 to 3 days, gently stirring on occasion to make sure the sugar dissolves into the vinegar. After this steeping period is over, strain the mixture through a fine-mesh strainer. The drinking vinegar syrup will keep, covered, in the refrigerator for at least 1 month.

COCKTAIL

Actually, I prefer to keep my drinking vinegar nonalcoholic because it's such a delightful and complex zero-proof option. Just add 1 ounce (30 ml) of drinking vinegar syrup to a tall ice-filled glass, top with soda water, stir gently, and serve.

CHANGE IT UP! You can use other ripe fruits instead of berries in this recipe, just chop them up well. You can also include a small handful of herbs with your berries while they steep with the sugar and vinegar to add complexity. Try mint, basil, or rosemary.

WILD HERBS

THERE IS A GRAND, HISTORIC TRADITION OF sticking wild herbs into alcohol, adding some sugar, and calling it medicinal. This is how many of the great aperitifs and digestifs came to be. Take Chartreuse, my spirit spirit. Green Chartreuse has 130 different botanicals macerated in it, which means that the French monks who first made it must have gone traipsing through the Alps near their monastery and added to it basically every wild herb that wouldn't outright kill them. And it's delicious.

FORAGED HERB LIQUEUR

MAKES 4 CUPS (960 ML)

To make your own modern take on Chartreuse, you will need to learn about the aromatic wild herbs that grow in your area. Some with a fairly wide range include pineapple weed (sometimes called wild chamomile), chamomile, wild mint, hyssop, angelica, chickweed, dandelion flowers, wood sorrel, mugwort, and wild bergamot. Then use them in this template.

1 tablespoon (about 8 g) chamomile or pineapple weed

½ teaspoon each of about 3 more wild herbs of your choice

1 teaspoon lemon balm or mint

½ teaspoon thyme

1 allspice berry

1 clove

¼ stick cinnamon

1 teaspoon lemon zest

2 cups (480 ml) vodka

¾ cup (150 g) sugar

¼ cup (85 g) honey

1½ cups (360 ml) water

Combine the chamomile, other wild herbs, lemon balm, thyme, allspice, clove, cinnamon, lemon zest, and vodka in a well-sealed container. Leave this to steep at room temperature for a week. Combine the sugar, honey, and water in a pot and heat, stirring, just until the sugar dissolves. Add this syrup to your herb and vodka mixture, reseal the container, and allow to steep for another 24 hours. Strain through a fine-mesh strainer lined with cheesecloth. The liqueur will keep almost indefinitely at room temperature in a sealed container.

FIELD AND GARDEN VERMOUTH

MAKES A GENEROUS 3 QUARTS (3 L)

Vermouth is another landing place for a huge variety of wild, medicinal, and obscure botanicals. When I first started researching to try to make my own vermouth about five years ago, I inadvertently found myself on an online forum for aspiring witches, if that tells you anything. Suffice it to say, if you have mugwort, wormwood, and blessed thistle, making vermouth is the very best, or at least the very best nonmagical, thing you can do with them. This makes a large batch, and that is because wormwood, the distinguishing feature of vermouth (vermouth comes from the word wermut, which means "wormwood" in German), is very hard to use in small batches. You can buy wormwood, gentian, and bitter orange peel from the website Mountain Rose Herbs.

Two 750 ml bottles dry white wine, divided

1½ teaspoons wormwood

½ teaspoon gentian

1 tablespoon (about 8 g) mixed foraged herbs

1-inch (2.5 cm) piece vanilla bean

1 tablespoon (8 g) bitter orange peel

6 rosemary leaves

3 sage leaves

¾ teaspoon thyme

3 cups (720 ml) tawny port

3 cups (600 g) sugar

1 cup (240 ml) water

2 cups (480 ml) brandy

In a heavy-bottomed pot, combine 1 bottle of the wine with the herbs and spices and bring just barely to a boil. Take off the heat and add the port. Cover the pot and put it in the refrigerator, leaving everything to infuse for 2 to 3 hours. Strain this mixture through a fine-mesh strainer lined with cheesecloth. Reserve the liquid. Next, combine the sugar and water in another heavy-bottomed pot. Cook over medium heat without disturbing until the sugar has caramelized to a dark amber color, 8 to 10 minutes.

Remove the sugar mixture from the heat and very carefully add the remaining bottle of wine. It will sputter like crazy from the heat, and the caramel will instantly seize up. Add the brandy as well, then return the pot to low heat and cook to let the seized-up caramel melt back in, stirring as needed. Combine the caramel mixture and the infused wine mixture. Divide among sealed bottles or jars. The vermouth will keep, stored in the refrigerator, for at least a month. Try it in any recipe that calls for sweet vermouth.

BAY LIQUEUR

Makes 4 cups (960 ml)

If you are lucky enough to live in an area such as the California coast where you can find bay laurel growing wild, you can use it on its own to make a gorgeous, complex liqueur that I think works beautifully in a Last Word cocktail (recipe below).

1 cup (about 100 g) fresh bay leaves

2 cups (480 ml) vodka

1 cup (200 g) sugar

1½ cups (360 ml) water

Combine the bay leaves and vodka in a well-sealed container and leave to steep at room temperature for 48 hours. Combine the sugar and water in a pot and heat, stirring, just until the sugar dissolves. Add this syrup to your bay and vodka mixture, reseal, and allow to steep for another 24 hours. Strain through a fine-mesh strainer lined with cheesecloth. The liqueur will keep almost indefinitely at room temperature in a sealed container.

COCKTAIL

To make a Last Word Cocktail, shake ¾ ounce (23 ml) gin, ¾ ounce (23 ml) Luxardo Maraschino liqueur, ¾ ounce (23 ml) Foraged Herb Liqueur or Bay Liqueur, 1 teaspoon simple syrup (see page 11), and ¾ ounce (23 ml) fresh lime juice with ice. Strain into a cocktail glass and garnish with a cherry.

FALL

AS L. M. MONTGOMERY WROTE IN *ANNE OF GREEN*
Gables, "I am so glad I live in a world where there are Octobers." I love the
electric colors, the expansive sky, and the feeling of nostalgia. I also love
the fruits of fall. Just as autumn is the time of abundant harvest on a farm,
it is a time of abundant harvest from the forest, as August's berries make
way for September and October's wild apples and rose hips.

WILD APPLES AND CRAB APPLES

IF YOU LIVE IN A COOL OR TEMPERATE CLIMATE AND you develop a habit of staring up into tree branches, you may be surprised by how often you stumble upon feral apple trees. Especially across New England and the Upper Midwest, the forests are dotted with remnants of former orchards and the offspring of apple seeds dropped here and there by animals, not to mention good old Johnny Appleseed. His aim was to propagate apples for making cider and applejack, not for eating, and most of the apples you find growing wild are tart, though there are exceptions.

Apples do not breed true. That is to say, apples cross-pollinate, causing the genetics in the seeds from a particular apple tree to be different from the genetics of the tree itself, and the apples growing from a parent tree's progeny will have their own grab bag of flavors, colors, and textures. (Commercial apple varieties are kept consistent by grafting.) They may not be the best for munching on, but wild apples can be delicious when roasted, and I particularly like to use them in infusions or for jelly. Wild crab apples are not actually a different species from apples. The term *crab* is just used to denote a particularly small size.

A FORAGER'S NOTE: Apple trees are usually medium-height, gnarled trees, and they have beautiful five-petal white blossoms in the spring. The fruit of feral trees is ready to pick in mid- to late fall and gets sweeter after the first frost. When you cut an apple in half horizontally, you should see five seeds arrayed in a starlike configuration.

WILD APPLE AND CRAB APPLE BITTERS

MAKES 1¼ CUPS (300 ML)

These gorgeous bitters are the perfect balance of fruity and aromatic. Like a pinch of salt and pepper in a cooking recipe, a dash or two of crab apple bitters lift and harmonize the flavors in a classic cocktail such as an Old Fashioned or a Manhattan.

1 cup (240 ml) bourbon, preferably barrel strength

1 cup (150 g) diced wild apples or crab apples (cut into 1-inch [2.5 cm] chunks or halved if small), seeds removed

1 tablespoon (9 g) dried sweet cherries

1 cinnamon stick, broken into a couple of chunks

Two 2-inch (5 cm)-long strips orange peel, removed with a vegetable peeler with no white pith

2 cloves

¼ teaspoon dried ginger

½ teaspoon coriander seeds

¼ teaspoon gentian root

½ cup (120 ml) water

1 tablespoon (15 ml) rich syrup (2 parts sugar dissolved in 1 part water)

Combine the bourbon, apples, cherries, cinnamon, orange peel, cloves, ginger, coriander, and gentian in a glass jar, cover, and let sit for 2 weeks. Strain through a fine-mesh strainer lined with cheesecloth, reserving what is left in the cheesecloth. Put the infused alcohol back into the jar. Next, transfer the spices and fruit that were left over in the cheesecloth to a pot and cover with the water. Simmer for 5 minutes. Strain the mixture through a fine-mesh strainer lined with cheesecloth, this time discarding what is left in the cheesecloth. Then add the strained, flavored water plus the rich syrup to the flavored alcohol in the jar. Store, sealed, at room temperature but out of the light, and your bitters should keep indefinitely.

Transfer your bitters to a dasher or dropper bottle and use to add an aromatic, autumnal lift to cocktails.

COCKTAIL

In an Old Fashioned glass, combine 1 teaspoon sugar, 1 teaspoon water, and 2 or 3 dashes of Wild Apple/Crab Apple Bitters. Stir to dissolve the sugar in the water, then add 2 ounces (60 ml) bourbon. Add a few ice cubes to your glass, stir for 15 to 20 seconds, then serve.

STAGHORN SUMAC

T O ME, STAGHORN SUMAC IS A RANGY-LOOKING TREE-BUSH THAT doesn't have a lot to recommend it most of the year. But all that changes when late summer or early fall comes around. The leaves blush to crimson, and the shrubs grow beautiful cones of fuzzy, Merlot-colored berries called sumac bobs. My friend Kelsey and I used to suck the acidity off of these tart berries, spitting out the middles as we walked through the woods. It's a fun pick-me-up while hiking, but if you can delay gratification and harvest some of the bobs to bring home, then you can make them into sumac tea. A couple of words to the wise: First, always steep your sumac in room-temperature water. Hot water pulls out intense bitterness. Also, staghorn sumac bobs will keep for months stored in a closed paper bag in a cool, dry place.

A FORAGER'S NOTE: there is a type of shrub called poison sumac, which does look somewhat like staghorn sumac but is actually more closely related to poison ivy. Poison sumac generally grows in wet, swampy areas; it has smooth edges on its leaves, whereas staghorn sumac has jagged-toothed edges; and, importantly, poison sumac does not produce red berries.

SUMAC TEA

Makes 2 cups (480 ml)

Sumac tea is a refreshing, traditional alternative to lemonade. It is a lovely shade of red, plus it's very high in vitamin C to help keep colds at bay.

2 cups (about 300 g) sumac berries

2 cups (480 ml) room-temperature water

2 tablespoons (25 g) sugar, or more to taste

In a container, combine the sumac berries and water, cover, and steep for 12 hours at room-temperature. Strain through a fine-mesh strainer. Stir in the sugar until it dissolves, then taste and add more sugar if desired. The sumac tea will keep, sealed and refrigerated, for about a week.

COCKTAIL

Combine 1½ ounces (45 ml) vodka and 6 ounces (180 ml) sumac tea in an ice-filled highball glass.

ROSE HIPS

ONE OF MY FAVORITE TREATS FROM CHILDHOOD was *nyppesuppe*, or rose-hip soup, which is a traditional Nordic dessert. Rose hips are the fruit of the rose bush that appear in the fall and hang onto the otherwise bare bushes late into the season. They are a stunning crimson or salmon orange, plump and rounded, with the withered flower sepals sticking out of their ends like fantastical little fairy crowns. And they are tasty, a combination of earthy and fruity and tart. You can eat rose hips raw, but they are filled with seeds, so you will want to cut them in half and use a small spoon to scoop them out—don't use your fingers, as the seeds are surrounded by tiny, very itchy hairs. I'm too lazy for this most of the time, so I use whole rose hips to make schnapps, simply straining out the spent hips.

A FORAGER'S NOTE: Almost all roses have hips that are usable. The type of rose that has the largest hips is the *Rosa rugosa*, also known as the salt spray rose (my favorite flower!). It can be found spreading into the wild in temperate climates, especially in coastal areas, but is mainly cultivated. However, roses cross-pollinate, so if you're lucky you may find wild roses that have cross-pollinated with rugosa and developed larger hips as a result. Even if you don't find them, using the hips for an infusion works beautifully with smaller varietals.

ROSE HIP SCHNAPPS

Makes 1½ cups (360 ml)

Rose Hip Schnapps makes for a nice sipping schnapps after a heavy meal. It reminds me a bit of rhubarb schnapps (which you can make using the same method) in the way it is tart but fruity at the same time; however, Rose Hip Schnapps has a richer, musky quality to it.

1 cup (about 150 g) rose hips

1½ cups (360 ml) vodka

Clean your rose hips and allow them to dry for 2 or 3 days somewhere out of the sun. Fill a jar two-thirds full with cleaned rose hips. Fill the jar with vodka to cover the rose hips. Seal and store in a cool, dark place for at least 1 month, shaking occasionally. Strain through a fine-mesh strainer lined with cheesecloth. Transfer to a clean jar or bottle. Allow to mellow for a couple more weeks before using.

TO TURN YOUR SCHNAPPS INTO A LIQUEUR: Add ½ cup (120 ml) of simple syrup for every 1 cup (240 ml) of schnapps. Allow to sit for 2 weeks before using.

COCKTAIL

Because rose hips and mint are a match made in heaven, try using your schnapps as the base spirit for a julep. Gently muddle 3 fresh mint leaves in the bottom of a julep cup. Add ½ ounce (15 ml) simple syrup (see page 11), 2 ounces (60 ml) Rose Hip Schnapps, ½ ounce (15 ml) bourbon, and a scoop of crushed ice. Stir gently, top with more crushed ice until it is slightly mounded over the top of your cup, then garnish with a small bouquet of more fresh mint leaves and a twist of lemon peel.

MOUNTAIN ASH BERRIES

WHENEVER I COME ACROSS A MOUNTAIN ASH tree in the fall, dripping with clusters of flaming red-orange berries, I want to plunk myself underneath it and stare up at it forever. They are so eye-catching, it is no wonder a wide variety of lore exists about them. The Vikings thought they were magical, and I rather think so myself. The beautiful berries are a favorite with birds, and, though bitter, they have long been used for making jellies and syrups in northern climes.

A FORAGER'S NOTE: Many people think that mountain ash berries (also known as rowan berries) are poisonous. They aren't poisonous, but they do contain parasorbic acid, which can make you sick in a large dose. However, cooking the berries converts the parasorbic acid into sorbic acid, which is safe.

MOUNTAIN ASH (ROWAN) BERRY SYRUP

MAKES 1 1/2 CUPS (360 ML)

The bittersweet and sour mountain ash berry reminds me a bit of cranberries on steroids. An easy syrup made from cooking the berries and adding sugar showcases their intense flavor in an approachable way and is a fun ingredient for adding wild flair to a drink. This syrup is especially tasty when used in drinks that combine it with other fall flavors such as apple, pear, cinnamon, nutmeg, and ginger.

1 cup (about 150 g) mountain ash berries

About 1 cup (240 ml) water

About 1 cup (200 g) sugar

Clean your mountain ash berries well, then add them to a saucepan and add enough water just to cover them. Bring to a boil, then lower the heat to a spirited simmer. Cook for 10 minutes, then use a spoon to gently smash the berries apart against the wall of your pot. Cook for another 10 to 15 minutes, until the berries are all falling apart. Remove from the heat and strain through a fine-mesh strainer lined with several layers of cheesecloth. You want to make sure that you are getting out all the little seeds in addition to the pulp.

Measure the amount of liquid you got and add an equal quantity of sugar (so, if you wind up with 1 cup [240 ml] of liquid after straining, add 1 cup [200 g] of sugar), and stir until the sugar dissolves. You should have a gorgeous red-orange syrup. Store in a sealed jar in the refrigerator for up to 2 weeks. Mountain ash berries are very high in pectin, so you may find that in the refrigerator your syrup turns to a sort of jelly. You can still use it; just loosen it up with a fork.

COCKTAIL

Add 1 ounce (30 ml) Mountain Ash (Rowan) Berry Syrup to a coupe glass and top with a dry hard cider.

RESOURCES

BARWARE AND BAR UTENSILS

Cocktail Kingdom
www.cocktailkingdom.com

OXO
www.oxo.com

Stanley flasks and thermoses
www.stanley-pmi.com

Nalgene bottles
www.nalgene.com

FORAGING

A Field Guide to Edible Wild Plants of Eastern and Central North America (Peterson Field Guide) by Lee Allen Peterson

Edible Wild Plants: A North American Field Guide to Over 200 Natural Foods by Thomas Elias and Peter Dykeman

The Skillful Forager: Essential Techniques for Responsible Foraging and Making the Most of Your Wild Edibles by Leda Meredith

Eat the Weeds
www.eattheweeds.com

Wild Edible
www.wildedible.com

COCKTAIL TECHNIQUE BOOKS

The Bar Book: Elements of Cocktail Technique by Jeffrey Morgenthaler

Death & Co: Modern Classic Cocktails by David Kaplan, Nick Fauchald, and Alex Day

Imbibe! by David Wondrich

Liquid Intelligence: The Art and Science of the Perfect Cocktail by Dave Arnold

ACKNOWLEDGMENTS

This book owes its existence to many wonderful people who I feel blessed to call my friends, family, and community. But there are a few who were so instrumental I literally could not have done it without them. Sherry, Mark, Kaitlin, Matti, and Jake, you are all epic. Thank you *so much* for your insights, your stories, your sweet modeling skills, and for letting me use all your camping gear that is just so much cuter and more photogenic than mine! Gudrun, thank you for letting me make an absolute mess of your kitchen and for being game to taste test any cocktail I sent your way, no matter the time of day. Thank you also to my darlings Chelsy and Caitlin, for gamely coming along on very cold photography trips to the woods and the lake and for eating hot dogs and kimchi with me after taking shots of fernet out of marshmallows. All in a day's work, I'd say. Hanna, thank you for your exquisite eye for light, detail, and movement and for making drinks look glamorous even when they were in camp cups and jars. I'm sorry we made you so frozen that you had to move to Portland to thaw out. Also, a huge thank you to Thom and the whole team at Quarto for handing over the reins and trusting Hanna's and my vision on this project.

Thank you to my amazing work family at Vikre Distillery! You are all rock stars, and every day you make it look like maybe Joel's and my crazy idea to start a distillery wasn't quite so crazy after all.

And above all, thank you to my family. Thank you, Mom and Dad, for bringing me up to be a creature of the forest as well as for all the millions of ways you've given me support and help. You're my greatest role models and inspirations, especially when it comes to noble, yet excessive, suffering. To Espen and Vidar, you are the lights of my life and quite possibly the cutest camping and cabin companions the world has ever seen. And Joel, you bought a flamethrower and melted ice off of the beach for me. If that's not true love, I don't know what is. Or else you just like flame throwing . . . Thank you for believing in me even more than I believe in myself, for helping me grow and push myself, and for accompanying me on this crazy expedition of life.

ABOUT THE AUTHOR

EMILY VIKRE is a native Duluthian who holds a PhD in food policy and behavioral theory from Tufts University. She is co-founder and co-owner of Vikre Distillery, which has been named best craft specialty spirits distillery by *USA Today*. The distillery has also won a slew of technical awards: a gold and five silvers at the San Francisco World Spirits Competition; gold, silver, and bronze awards from the American Craft Distiller's Association; silvers and bronze from the American Distilling Institute; and two Good Food awards. A nationally recognized food and drinks writer, Emily has been a regular columnist for *Food52*, and has written for *Lucky Peach*, Minnesota Public Radio, and *Norwegian American Weekly*. When she isn't at work, you'll find her forest bathing, foraging, and cross-country skiing along the North Shore of Lake Superior with her husband, two young sons, and adorable mutt, Squid.

INDEX